THE TIMES EDUCATIONAL SUPPLEMENT

SCHOOL LEADERSHIP

NATIONAL &

INTERNATIONAL

PERSPECTIVES

EDITED BY
JOHN DUNFORD • RICHARD FAWCETT
& DAVID BENNETT

KOGAN PAGE

First published in 2000 by Kogan Page Limited
Reprinted 2001

Kogan Page Limited
120 Pentonville Road
London N1 9JN
UK

British Library Cataloguing in Publication Data

A CIP record for this book is available from the British Library.

ISBN 0 7494 3384 1

Typeset by D & N Publishing, Baydon, Wiltshire
Printed and bound in Great Britain by Clays Ltd, St Ives plc

Contents

Contents

Contributors

David Bennett: Policy consultant to the Secondary Heads Association (SHA). Formerly, principal, Sackville Community College, East Grinstead, West Sussex, UK

Jill Clough: Head teacher, East Brighton College of Media Arts. Formerly, head teacher, Wimbledon High School, Wimbledon, London, UK

Maureen Cruickshank: Head teacher, Beauchamp Community College, Oadby, Leicestershire, UK

Paul Desmet: Head teacher, Lyceum O.L.V. ter – Nieuwe-Plant, Ieper, Belgium

Michael Doig: Head teacher, Cumbernauld High School, Cumbernauld, North Lanarkshire, Scotland, UK

John Dunford: General Secretary of the Secondary Heads Association, Leicester, UK. Formerly head teacher of Durham Johnston Comprehensive School, Durham, UK

Richard Fawcett: Head teacher, Thurston Community College, Thurston, Suffolk, UK

Mike Hardacre: Director, Wolverhampton Education Action Zone, West Midlands. Formerly, head teacher, Coppice Community High School, Wolverhampton, West Midlands, UK

Mary Jarvis: Principal, Smoky Hill High School, Englewood, Colorado, USA

Clive Minnican: Head teacher, St Matthew's Primary School, Ipswich, Suffolk, UK

Chris Nicholls: Head teacher, Moulsham High School, Chelmsford, Essex, UK

Allan Peachey: Principal, Rangitoto College, North Shore City, New Zealand

Chris Plant: Principal, Musgrave Hill School, Southport, Queensland, Australia

Michael Pritchard: Head teacher, Langley Moor Primary School, Durham, UK

Marc Sackur: President, Lycée Lakanal, Paris, France

Foreword

Over the past 15 years, the British education system has come under increasing pressure to raise standards of achievement – especially in schools that traditionally have taken some of the most difficult pupils. This means that the role of the head teacher as a leader is becoming ever more crucial. As I write this foreword, the first £90,000-a-year maintained-school head has just been appointed; how long before the first six-figure salary for the leader of a school? Only three years ago, when Labour came to power with its pledge to keep education high on the political agenda, the idea of such salaries would have been out of this world. But the drive to improve the achievement of all our young people has highlighted the fact that this cannot be done without leadership which is clear, focused, and, above all, inspiring.

Whichever party is in power, schooling is now a high-profile policy issue, so it is not surprising that head teachers, as the people in the front line, are under heavy pressure to deliver. Today's heads have to be experts in public relations, leading from the front, managing and appraising staff, choosing computer systems, working in partnership with governors, understanding the complexities of performance-related pay, and selecting the management team to help them run the place. If they are out of their depth in any of these, then they have to know someone who can offer sound advice.

All heads suffer from exposure because, within each school, the buck stops with them. All their activities take place in the spotlight, and the pressure comes both from within and from without. Heads in the private sector have always known this, but throughout the system, today's schools are run much more like businesses than in the days when local authorities could say that they stamped a distinctive mark on the institutions in their area.

Many head teachers have adopted the language, the methods and even the dress of the business world – but often without sufficient training in the complexities of their task. No wonder the last four years have seen strenuous but not always successful attempts to ensure an adequate programme of preparation is devised. The new national college for leadership at Nottingham is offering some useful insights and answers, and through the Internet we can at last see some joined-up thinking on the nature and practice of leadership extending right across the country.

But, while understanding school leadership – as well as discussion and the sharing of ideas – is crucial if head teachers are to develop their practice in a thoughtful and effective manner, there is no substitute for experience. Theories have a way of requiring rapid modification when put to the test of real life. In an atmosphere of rapid change and information overload, it is reassuring to have some trustworthy constants to fall back on. This compendium of individual head teachers' experiences, selected from different age groups and countries, and edited by three of the most respected practitioners in the field, offers aspirant heads some thought-provoking examples of good practice which might act as stepping stones across some of the turbulent waters they are entering. And serving heads will find in this book some rich material for reflection – as they consider, doubtless not for the first time or last time, the nature of successful leadership.

Caroline St John-Brooks
Editor, The Times Educational Supplement

INTRODUCTION

A search for the generic attributes of successful leadership is a quest for the impossible. Although the term exists in any self-respecting dictionary, the qualities necessary to exercise such a role are multiple and varied. In a recent book on leadership, *Leading Minds* (Gardner, 1996), the author tells the stories of 11 world leaders, but makes no attempt to propose the generic attributes of their leadership. He confines himself to the 'principal dimensions' of the role. Even if the context is restricted to school leadership, the task of defining generic attributes from the literature remains a hopeless task.

Yet everyone agrees that effective leadership is one of the most important factors in the success of a school. In 1988 the House of Commons Select Committee on Education, a committee drawn from all the main political parties, investigated the role of head teacher. In the conclusion to its report, the committee commented that 'there seems to be a very high degree of correlation between the behaviour of the head teacher and the progress and achievement of the people inside the school' (House of Commons, 1998). Styles of leadership vary greatly: autocratic, democratic, liberal, consensus and consultative are all adjectives used to describe different styles. Ultimately, style is less important than impact, effectiveness and fitness for purpose. Some might argue that democratic is a better style than autocratic because it places a greater value on the involvement of others. 'Surely this places the greatest importance on the humanity of the individual,' they might claim. 'Not necessarily so' could be the reply.

All effective leaders use a range of styles on a regular basis, seeking to fit each to the purpose of the activity. There is no place for democracy when evacuating the school in an emergency, when autocracy must reign. Likewise, when taking a decision that directly affects the working conditions of staff, their views must be taken into account. Democracy and consultation will have a greater role to play.

Few doubt the assertion that the role of head teacher is very demanding and is becoming even more so. Nor do many doubt that when the role is undertaken well, the effective head is one of the best examples of leadership. In providing evidence for the Select Committee referred to above, Hay McBer Ltd, the international management consultants, commented that 'highly effective head teachers were the highest performing leaders when compared to other groups of senior managers in public and private sector organizations' (House of Commons, 1998). In the same evidence they added that 'the role of the head is one of the most demanding that they have ever encountered because of the sheer range of management and leadership accountabilities'.

In writing about effective school leadership, no attempt has been made in this book to identify generic qualities or to focus on particular styles. Both tasks would be fruitless. Each head teacher has been left to tell his or her own story and to conclude with reflections about individual style. Readers must be left to draw their own conclusions about the relationship between style and effectiveness. It is the stories themselves that will provide the basis for their judgements.

LEADERSHIP AND MANAGEMENT

Both leadership and management are necessary for a school to be effective. Each must be present, but they are quite separate in their meaning. In short, leadership is the ability to move the school forward, whilst management is concerned with the procedures necessary to keep the school running. Leadership is concerned with the long term and the strategic, management with the immediate and short term. Vision is articulated and set by the leader, whilst the manager is required to design and implement procedures which enable the vision to be achieved.

An effective head teacher needs to be both a leader and a manager. The head must ensure that: good communication systems are in place; expectations are clear and consistently applied; procedures are unambiguous and fit for purpose; policies are articulated and appropriate; and that the implementation of all these is monitored and evaluated. Management can, however, and in many cases should, be delegated to other senior members of staff. Aspects of leadership can also be delegated, but primarily it must ultimately remain the responsibility of the head teacher.

If the head teacher is not exercising effective leadership, or if the head focuses on the management task alone, then one of two alternatives will occur. Firstly, the school may drift. The analogy of a ship without steering is graphic. The ship has no direction, it might go in circles, arrive at the wrong destination or, worse still, it could destroy itself on the rocks. Alternatively, the absence of leadership from the top may mean that it is exercised by others. There are likely to be a number of interested parties ready to step into the vacuum. Under such circumstances, leadership may be grasped by a coterie of staff or governors or even a powerful individual. Such action will lead staff, students, parents and governors, to ask the question: 'Who's in charge?' Anarchy is only just below the surface with any group and it surfaces quickly in the absence of effective leadership. The ultimate power of a vortex depends on the size of the hole, but unless the vacuum is filled, chaos may reign.

It is leadership, rather than management, that will remain the focus of the contributions to this book. Management, whilst important, will be left to the writing of others. Before proceeding, a brief look at the historical development of the leadership role in schools will set the context for understanding the current and some of the future requirements of such a position.

HISTORICAL DEVELOPMENT

The earliest examples of schools as we know them, in the 14th and 15th centuries, had a head teacher at the helm. Each was a social institution with someone in charge. This model continued with the introduction of public education in the United Kingdom during the 19th century. The head teacher was seen as the leader of the institution who exercised some responsibility for the setting and implementation of standards. Schools were simple institutions whose task was to teach. During the first part of the 20th century, more began to be expected and, as a result, the role of head teacher became more complex.

The head might occasionally be absent and, in any event, it was impossible for one person to meet all the expectations of the role. Deputies were appointed, largely to deputize for the head teacher and to undertake delegated responsibilities. By the late 1950s the typical British deputy head teacher in a secondary school would have been responsible for the construction of the weekly timetable and ensuring that the school operated efficiently on a day-to-day basis. In addition, the individual retained a substantial teaching load. Primary schools too had begun to appoint deputy heads, in order to cope with their increase in size and public expectations.

By the early 1970s, schools were quite different places. Many had increased significantly in size, most had been affected by the move to comprehensive education and public expectations had increased still further. All but the smallest primary schools had appointed a deputy and many secondary schools had two, three or even four such positions. This was to change still further in the late 1980s with the introduction in England and Wales of Local Management of Schools (LMS). The view was increasingly taken that detailed decision-making should be delegated to those who were closest to its impact. Similar moves were occurring in the United States, Australia and New Zealand, though not in many parts of Europe. Thus the introduction of LMS as part of the 1988 Education Act required that every school in England and Wales should be responsible for its own budgeting in relation to staffing, teaching resources and the tenant responsibilities for the building. Simultaneously, schools were permitted to apply to government for the direct control of all of their finances. In short, the money followed the student and the range of responsibilities increased accordingly. As a result, the concept of the leadership team began to emerge.

LEADERSHIP TEAMS

The concept and practice of a senior management team (SMT) is not new. As schools increased in size and complexity, the need for delegated decision-making from the head teacher to senior managers and for the co-ordination of whole school roles became self-evident. From the early 1970s secondary schools began to see the role of the SMT as a critical aspect of their decision-making structure. Quite often the head teacher shared the responsibility for taking decisions and the SMT in turn accepted corporate responsibility. Where a school had more than one deputy, each had a different role. Effective schools ensured that the roles were distinct from each other, with each having a clear rationale for the range of the post-holder's remit. It is interesting to note, however, that as late as 1990 a survey by the Secondary Heads Association (SHA) discovered that many deputy heads still had little more than a list of tasks gathered over a number of years (SHA, 1990). During the same period many primary schools also established a management team, usually consisting of those who held additional responsibilities for co-ordinating elements of the curriculum.

Most SMTs were true to their name. That is to say, the roles held by members were largely defined as management tasks. How do we deal with this matter of discipline? What should be our policy on mobile telephones? Who should lead this working party of staff? All important questions, but largely ones that concerned the day-to-day working of the school. With the introduction of LMS and a further increase in delegated responsibilities, this pattern is changing again, both in the United Kingdom and in a number of other countries. An additional critical factor has been the gradual emergence of a focus on the effectiveness of teaching and learning, together with the learning needs of the individual child. These extra dimensions, central to the core role of the school, are having a far-reaching effect on the way schools are led and managed.

The recent emergence of the term 'leadership team' is therefore no accident. If schools, particularly secondaries, are to be effective in the future, executive authority will need to be delegated by the head teacher to senior colleagues. Whilst the head will remain the leader, others will need to add a leadership role to their management responsibilities. Although the authors commissioned the following chapters from head teachers, they are aware that many of the characteristics must apply to deputy head teachers and other senior leaders if schools are to be effective in the future. They are committed to the concept and practice of the leadership team and trust that much of the material in this book will also contribute to the development of the roles of deputy and assistant head teacher.

THE RIGHT PLACE AND TIME

Sir Winston Churchill was a classic example. His leadership of the British nation during the Second World War was instrumental in achieving success. Yet, immediately after the war the British nation voted Churchill and his party out of office. Whilst it might be simplistic to conclude that the people had judged his leadership to be suitable for war but not for peace, most would agree that when he became Prime Minister again in 1950 his leadership was not particularly noteworthy. In short, effective leadership by a particular individual can depend on being in the right place at the right time.

Professor John MacBeath draws a similar conclusion when he says 'from our study of leadership a good head in school A may, when she moves to school B, become a good head in an entirely different way, or might not be such a good head at all' (MacBeath, 1999). In fact not only may the context and time be critical factors in effective headship, but if appointed to another post an entirely different range of skills may well be needed. The exercise of effective leadership in an inner-city school will not, of itself, fit the individual for such leadership in a county town. Likewise to parachute in a successful head from a leafy suburb in order to solve the problems of a failing school could result in further decline for the school. Fitness for purpose is of crucial importance. In considering the case studies, the context will be just as important to understand as the style or challenge.

LEADERSHIP TRAINING

Few countries offer extensive training to school leaders. France is one of the exceptions, but their system is centralized and head teachers are employed as civil servants. There is little scope for local decision-making and the delegation of resources which has occurred in the United Kingdom, Australia and New Zealand has yet to be implemented. Elsewhere, systematic school leadership programmes are emerging, but they are in their infancy.

In the last five years of the 20th century, a structured leadership programme emerged piecemeal in England. There are now three strands: the National Professional Qualification for Heads (NPQH); the Headship Leadership and Management Programme (HEADLAMP); and the Leadership Programme for Serving Heads (LPSH). Furthermore, by 2002, government intention is that NPQH will be a prerequisite for all head teacher appointments. The programme, which contains a number of core elements, is delivered in full to all participants. HEADLAMP, the oldest of the three strands, is different and works on a deficit model. The starting point is a series of characteristics in which an effective head teacher would expect to be proficient. Through a self-evaluation exercise, or with the support of a consultant, the newly appointed head identifies the characteristics that are in need of development. A programme to meet the need is designed and implemented over a two-year period. LPSH is for head teachers who have been in post for more than five years. A range of mechanisms – 360 degree appraisal, a residential assessment centre and the use of a mentor – all contribute to the further development of experienced heads.

These programmes will become the core, but not the sole, activity of the National College for School Leadership (NCSL) in Nottingham, England. Much is expected of the college by the profession, politicians and increasingly the public. It will not be able to meet all these aspirations, but school leaders in particular have welcomed its formation. There are moves in other countries to establish similar centres, but England is leading the world in this respect. The SHA delegation, which hosted an invitation seminar at the annual conference of the International Confederation of Principals (ICP) in Helsinki in July 1999, was inundated by interest in the college from the 25 nations involved. At one of the early planning seminars, in the autumn of the same year, which brought together educational academics from Australia, Canada and the United States, the international participants declared the initiative to be the most important development in school leadership at the start of the new millennium. 'The eyes of the educational world will be on this initiative. It's a world first.'

INTERNATIONAL DIMENSION

We live in an international world. The emergence of widespread, commercial air travel in the second half of the last century, and latterly the development of communications technology, have combined to shrink the global exchange of ideas and knowledge. Leaders need to learn from the good practice of others, wherever that is taking place. Some will have the privilege of an international visit in order to learn at first hand. Others will do so through electronic means such as the online service operated by the ICP or the Department for Education and Employment's (DfEE) international Web site. Many more will do so through the stories of leaders and their schools across the globe. It will be part of the remit for the NCSL to provide access to learning from international contexts, as well as contributing to the development of educational leaders in other countries. Maintaining that vision during the early stages will ensure that the college makes a unique contribution to the development of school leadership.

Schools should also be preparing children and young people to be citizens of the international community. Nobody can be certain of what the implication will be for those now in school, but current and future school leaders owe it to their students to learn the lessons of good practice from around the world in order to equip young people for future citizenship.

CONCLUSION

Whatever the future holds for school leaders, change and uncertainty will be ever present. The Royal Society of Arts (RSA) has done much to foster the debate about the future of work and education. In the compendium, *On Work and Leadership* (RSA, 1999), Hillary Cropper, chief executive of the FI Group, comments:

> In these times of rapid development and global interaction, stability is an illusion. The organization is either going forwards or backwards; it is getting better or

worse; it is gaining ground or losing it. It cannot stand still. If the person at the top does not create change, then by definition that person is not a leader.

In his own chapter, Philip Hodgson of the Ashridge Management College comments:

> One of the important underlying themes for leadership is that of handling the increased uncertainty associated with increased choice.'

This book sets out to illustrate the practice of effective school leadership, from a variety of British and international contexts, at a time when the service is facing unprecedented change and uncertainty. The contributions are designed to illustrate many styles of leadership, each tailored to the context of a particular school. The launch of the National College for School Leadership will further raise the profile of this topic. To that end, it is the editors' firm conviction that this publication will not only celebrate the excellence of school leadership, but will provide important and informed evidence for those who ask 'what makes a school leader successful?'

REFERENCES

Gardner, H (1996) *Leading Minds: An anatomy of leadership*, Harper Collins, London

House of Commons (1998) *The Role of Head Teachers*, The Stationery Office, Norwich

MacBeath, J (1999) *Schools Must Speak for Themselves*, Routledge, London

Royal Society of Arts (1999) *On Work and Leadership*, Gower, London

Secondary Heads Association (1990) *If it Moves*, SHA, Leicester

1

Leading with a dream

ALLAN PEACHEY

My entire teaching career has been in state co-educational Year 9–13 (ages 12–18) secondary schools. Since 1993 I have been principal of Rangitoto College, New Zealand's largest school with a roll of 2500 students. Before that, three years were spent as principal and one as deputy principal at Colenso High School, Napier. After gaining an MA degree in history from the University of Canterbury, the early years were spent as head of commerce at Naenae College, Lower Hutt and 12 years as an assistant teacher of history and economics at Hutt Valley High School. I served as the elected president of the Secondary Principals Association of New Zealand from 1998 to 2000.

RANGITOTO COLLEGE

Rangitoto College is a state secondary school located in North Shore City, 15 kilometres north of Auckland City. Its socio-economic context is that of a decile 10 school. Every New Zealand state school is assigned a decile, a 10 per cent grouping, based on the degree of disadvantage of the community from which students are drawn. Rangitoto College draws its students from communities with the

9

lowest degree of socio-economic disadvantage. In contrast, Colenso High School had a decile 3 rating putting it in the category of schools that draw students from communities with the highest degree of socio-economic disadvantage.

Although the community from which Rangitoto College draws its students contains the full socio-economic spectrum, the majority of families lie in the middle to upper-middle bracket. Employment statistics for the local community show that more than a third of the work force are classified as 'technical and professional' or 'administration and managerial'. Over a third of the college's parent community have a post-secondary school qualification. The community is predominantly Caucasian with a very small Maori and Pacific Island population. The number of immigrant families in the community, particularly from Asia and South Africa, has increased over the last decade.

PORTRAIT OF THE COLLEGE IN 1993

Rangitoto College was highly regarded in 1993 as a successful school that had been well led by its previous principals. Some may have said that it was at risk of becoming a coasting school. Early impressions did suggest that the college was a little reluctant to take the final steps towards being the best school in its community because it did not want to be seen as better than or different from surrounding schools.

1993 was the early days of what was known in New Zealand as the 'Tomorrow's Schools' reforms. The administration of the compulsory education sector had been the subject of a review 'Administering for Excellence'. Out of this came a revised Education Act that gave more flexibility and independence to schools than they had ever had before and introduced the concept of local governance. Trustees, elected by a school's parent community, were to govern schools while principals were to lead and manage. The paternal Department of Education, a bureaucratic icon of a bygone age, was closed on 30 September 1989. The following Monday the Ministry of Education opened, primarily as a policy unit to advise government.

At the heart of the change was financial independence for schools. In the first year of Tomorrow's Schools nearly NZ $450 million was handed directly to schools in operational funding. After 10 years of the project that figure now exceeds NZ $1 billion, of which NZ $680 million is operational funding and NZ $400 million is bulk-funded teachers' salaries for nearly 35 per cent of the schools with devolved funding, schools that educate 41 per cent of the student population. Local governance was a huge vote of confidence in the ability of schools, and their communities, to make the best decisions, and to operate in the most effective ways for the good of their students.

The college has had four principals since it opened in 1956. The conventional wisdom of the community is that each principal has been 'incredibly appropriate for their time and all have added much to the school'. The second and third principals were both outstanding 'systems' people who had been very successful and highly respected within the centralized bureaucratic structures of the old Department of Education. They knew how things were done and the college benefited from that. The developments of 1993 were new to this generation. Local governance put a premium, not on a system-orientated approach, but on the need for principals to exploit an environment that required them to get outside the system. They needed to consider innovative means of achieving the school's potential, by using the flexibility and independence of Tomorrow's Schools. Principals had to be entrepreneurial. They were encouraged to take risks and strong communication skills were required. Communities had a real sense of ownership of their schools.

Shortly before my appointment, the board of trustees surveyed the community to measure its impression of the performance of the college. There were very strong approval ratings for all aspects of its operation, with particularly strong support for the academic emphasis. Parents did, however, say that they would like to see a greater emphasis on careers and vocational education. They expressed a desire for as much information as possible about what was going on at the college. Parents also wanted to feel welcome at the school and to be involved, particularly when difficulties arose. In the total context of the college and of its high approval ratings, parents saw these as relatively minor points. In fact they were significant in terms of the requirements imposed by the Tomorrow's Schools initiative in responding to the needs of the community.

SIGNIFICANT CHANGES AND CHALLENGES

By 1993, Rangitoto College was on the threshold of significant roll growth. It was housing 1650 students in permanent buildings adequate for 1000. The overflow was housed in some 30 transportable classrooms, many of old design and in poor condition. Research indicated that year after year the college's roll had exceeded official projections. This was despite the contraction of its enrolment boundaries and the establishment of other secondary schools in adjacent suburbs. The official Department of Education view had been that the roll would peak during the 1980s and fall back to 1200 by the early 1990s. Land that the Department of Education had owned for another secondary school, a few blocks from the college, had been sold as surplus to requirements. By 1993 what had been seen as a temporary situation was rapidly becoming a major challenge. Rolls in contributing primary schools were on the rise, infill housing was bringing more teenagers into the area and a population influx from Asia and South Africa was adding to the growth.

Two things were apparent. First, the college's roll would continue to be under pressure. It would no longer be possible to hold the numbers at 1650, let alone reduce to 1200. Other local secondary schools were facing the same pressures. This was not a case of one school wanting more students at another's expense. Several schools each needed to take their share of the increase. Secondly, centralized government planning for the provision of school places had been found seriously wanting. There was no provision for another school to be built quickly.

For some this was a problem; others seized it as an opportunity. The leadership of Rangitoto College took the initiative. They negotiated with the Ministry of Education for the provision of further school places. A roll growth strategy was developed that would see this and other schools resourced with further property provisions in return for taking extra students. Rangitoto College agreed with the Ministry of Education to increase its roll from 1650 to 2500.

The agreement resulted in a major rebuilding of the college and provided the opportunity to rethink curriculum delivery, student management and the leadership and organizational systems. The first priority was to decide whether curriculum delivery or student management should be the college's focus. In the light of its academic tradition and in acknowledgement of the results of the community survey, the decision was easy. The college would continue to be structured around curriculum delivery and the student management services were to ensure that the curriculum achievement was at the highest standard.

An extensive building programme dealt with the need for extra classrooms and provided the redesign for the infrastructure necessary for a school of 2500 students. At the same time the opportunity was taken to remove the majority of the temporary classrooms from the site. Underpinning the redevelopment was the opportunity to centralize each curriculum area around its head of department. This would facilitate the development of a leadership rather than managerial style amongst heads of departments. A statement was also made about the value that the college places on its teaching staff. Each teacher was provided with a personal workspace of a standard that they could expect if they were working in an open area in a government department or a medium-sized business.

The biggest challenge of all was to decide how the college should be led and managed. Leadership now resides in the hands of the principal, while management is left to an associate principal, supported by a team of three deputy principals and three assistant principals. One deputy is responsible for curriculum and assessment, another for student management and a third for operational matters. The three assistant principals have overlapping functions supporting the deputy principals. In a school of 2500 it is vital to have depth at every layer of the system. Each day a deputy and an assistant principal lead a group of teachers responsible for the supervision of the campus. They are the front line in dealing with whatever issues arise during the day.

Behind the focus on curriculum delivery is a team of four guidance counsellors, two careers counsellors and a learning support team. Their prime responsibility is to ensure a pastoral and guidance environment in the college that emphasizes the positive qualities of learning. It also needs to deal with those barriers that interrupt the individual progress of students and which, on occasions, can interrupt the learning of whole classes.

In 1995 Rangitoto College was one of a dozen very large schools faced with a potential staffing crisis that proved to be a major test of leadership skills. The 12 largest schools in New Zealand were to face government-imposed staffing cuts. At the college, 16 middle-management staff faced demotion and loss of salary. If the cuts were not accepted, the only alternative was the introduction of a bulk-fund for teachers' salaries.

As part of the Tomorrow's Schools reforms, one of the cornerstones of self-management had been to bulk-fund salaries. Schools were to receive entitlement funding from government to pay the salaries of teachers. The school would decide how many teachers it would employ and what its management structures would be. Initially the scheme did not proceed because of strong opposition by the teachers' unions. When government changed in 1990, the new administration decided that the opportunity to bulk-fund should be an option for individual school boards. By 1995 a number of schools had taken up the option, but most had done so in an environment of extreme hostility from the teachers' unions. Many of the extra-curricular programmes in such schools had suffered from the withdrawal of support by teachers. A number of the principals of the early bulk-funded schools became the subject of severe criticism and, in some cases, ostracism by the teachers' unions and by fellow principals.

As a result of the threatened cuts, the principals of the large schools began to look seriously at bulk-funding for the first time. Rangitoto College moved quickly to open a discussion with its staff on the planned cuts in staffing and on the availability of bulk-funding as a solution. There was, within the staff, some opposition to the concept, but the great majority were prepared to be open minded and to consider all the issues on their merits. A principal's leadership in such a situation is critical to a successful outcome. It was essential to understand the deep-seated opposition that the teachers' unions had to bulk-funding and the traditional suspicion that teachers have for government. Members of the teaching staff needed time and space to form their own view on the issue. Over a period of months staff attitudes to bulk-funding shifted markedly. It was important for me to be totally honest about my own thinking and in confronting the concerns of others.

Informal discussions were held with individuals and small groups while support for a move into bulk-funding was built. Gradually a consensus emerged that the principal and the board of trustees could be trusted to make the best decision for the college. While the matter was being considered by teaching staff, the board of trustees, whose chairman wisely insisted on a unanimous decision, was also considering the issue. During this consensus-building exercise everyone was free to express their views, to change their opinions and to ask whatever questions they wanted, without any concern of recrimination from the college leadership or from their colleagues.

When the board finally made the decision to bulk-fund, I advised the staff of the fact and of what it meant for the future. Quick delivery of the benefits to staff was essential. It had also been essential to insist that the board's resolution to enter bulk-funding included a commitment that all monies handed over by government for teachers' salaries were to be spent only on teachers' salaries. That commitment alone gave confidence to the teaching staff.

Bulk-funding later became a significant instrument in the management of the roll growth that was occurring. The only legal requirement imposed on a bulk-funded school was that it must have a principal and a sufficient number of teachers to deliver the curriculum. Following the agreement to increase the roll I had insisted that the property resources needed for growth should be put in place in advance of the roll growth. This was not to be a catch-up exercise. Teachers, students and the community were to have a sense of the college moving forward, not a sense of overcrowding and crisis. In the same way, the flexibility available from bulk-funding was used to put in place the staffing structures needed for a growing school in advance of the arrival of the extra students. This would not have been possible under a centralized staffing system that required the students to be in the school, application to be made for further staffing and the approvals given, before additional staff could be appointed. As a result we were appointing staff four months before the start of the year, thus not waiting until the year had started and playing catch-up.

PRESENT STATE OF THE COLLEGE

The growth of the college roll was led in such a way as to minimize its impact. Staff, students and parents were given a sense that the college was getting better all the time. The present state was fairly summarized by the most recent Accountability

Review Report issued by the Education Review Office. It concluded that the strong 'Rangi' culture provides a climate where mutual respect between staff and students is the norm. Visionary leadership was judged as underpinning the strong sense of purposefulness and energy in the school. Students and staff were recognized as being proud of their school and shared a commitment to achieving high standards.

It was noted that, since the 1995 review, the school had begun a phase of well-managed growth associated with a substantial increase in the roll. Recent developments had included the provision of improved facilities for teaching English, science, art, mathematics and technology, and the recruitment of high-quality staff.

The board was complimented on having effectively managed the changes associated with the continuing growth of the school. It was also well placed to cope with the planned future roll of 2500. The review team noted that a number of factors had contributed to the promotion of high standards of student achievement at Rangitoto College during the period of school growth. These included the high quality of educational leadership, school culture, learning support, pastoral care and parental involvement.

The principal, senior managers and heads of department were considered to provide strong educational leadership. Their high expectations of teacher and student performance were clearly expressed. The relationship between the senior managers and staff was helpful and supportive. Teachers reported a strong sense of direction, collegiality, trust and commitment.

Curriculum management systems were considered to be well established. A variety of effective approaches were being used to ensure that the quality of the teaching programmes was maintained at a high level. Heads of department provided good quality leadership and there were clear guidelines for teachers about what was expected of them. Curriculum managers closely monitored the work of their staff and students and provided additional guidance when appropriate.

Today, teachers work together to plan and evaluate their programmes and actively share their educational ideas. Those with expertise are encouraged to share their knowledge with colleagues. This fosters the development of a professional culture within the school. Teachers take pride in their work and this motivates students to do likewise.

LEADERSHIP STYLE

Following the Tomorrow's Schools reforms of 1989, the nature of principalship in New Zealand changed. Many took the opportunity to throw off the shackles of management for genuine educational leadership. The role can now be defined in two parts, as the instructional leader of the school, and as the chief executive to the board of trustees.

A principal must be able to do both well. It cannot be said that one is more important than the other. The inability to perform as chief executive to the board will undermine the ability to provide instructional leadership. It is the board that sets policy and the principal who advises it. His job is then to lead the implementation of the policy decisions. Underpinning effective principalship is the responsibility to manage the relationship with integrity. One of the greatest satisfactions of the role is that of knowing that the key relationships have been got right. Do this, and a lot of other things fall into place.

Accepting roll growth and the bulk-funding of teachers' salaries marked significant changes for Rangitoto College. The challenges arising from these changes provide a framework to illustrate the development of my leadership style. The objective of the change was to ensure that the college would be a better school for having increased its size and for having changed the method by which its teachers' salaries are funded. How does a principal take a school which is already doing well and move it beyond its comfort zones, but in such a way that tensions or anxieties are not created? At the same time, it was important to create a sense of urgency to ensure that change was not rendered ineffective through the complacency of staff, thereby negating the objective of ensuring that Rangitoto College would be a better school.

Bulk-funding could not have been introduced just because I thought it was a good idea. One person alone, however influential, cannot overcome opposition from the body of teachers. The consensus of acceptance that was established was beyond the capability of one person. It needed other senior managers, heads of curriculum areas and teachers working in the same direction. Some would, of course, be quicker to buy into change than others.

Schools are complex systems of people, curriculum, assessment, reporting, conflicting values and even clashes of cultures. To be effective they need to be well managed, but to excel they need to be led. Those who choose only to manage surrender leadership to others. Principals who lead let others manage. Leadership of a school is about providing vision, about establishing what the future will be like and then winning support for the vision from those who can make it happen. Schools whose principal does not lead will get stranded in complacency, problems will not be confronted and solved, and opportunities will be missed. Leadership in schools means seizing opportunities, confronting problems and always seeking to improve. The challenge facing many principals is to move out of a management mode and into leadership.

Those who take on the management mode alone may enjoy success within the narrow confines of the definitions of management. They have plans and they might even have timetables for achieving their plans, but they do not have the vision that will enable their schools to fly. They do not think strategically to produce the changes needed to realize the vision. Genuinely successful principals are leaders from day one. In fact, the best will have been leaders before they become principals. They may have come through schools that have cultivated leadership at all levels within the organization. They will have learned from principals who have encouraged them to have visions and to take risks. Rather than be punished for making mistakes they will have been expected to learn from their mistakes. They will understand management and they will have managed successfully, but they will, in particular, have developed that attribute of always looking to extend their management responsibility into a leadership role. The more that the principal is the leader of the school and the more others exercise leadership, the stronger the school will be.

It took leadership to accept the opportunities of roll growth, to rebuild and refocus Rangitoto College. It took leadership to seize the opportunity of bulk-funding. Leadership involves risk-taking. The risks in growing the roll and in adopting a funding mechanism for teachers' salaries, which was widely disliked by the teachers' unions, meant pushing beyond old safety zones into systems that were new and different. For principals to be successful as leaders they must be prepared to take risks. The risks are less if the vision is sound and if there is a capacity to generate confidence in that vision. Leadership risks can be minimized when people who will be affected by change are listened to and minds are kept open to the views of others. Rangitoto College was led into roll growth and bulk-funding, not managed into it.

Principals need passion for their schools and for their jobs. They must be constantly reaching out to as many people as they can. Staff, students and parents need to share the vision and spread the passion. Time must be made for talking to people and for mentoring. Routine paper tasks are of no significance when set against getting human relationships right. Thinking leadership, rather than management, changes the dynamics by which a principal can deal with people.

Principals should lead their schools by walking around them regularly. They should move around with the calm confidence of someone in total control. Their eyes and ears will be open and they will spend a lot of time listening, praising, encouraging and acknowledging. Every opportunity will be taken to talk to staff rather than communicating by way of paper or electronic means. Go to where the teachers are working and share their workspace with them. Take every opportunity to be seen in the school's community. Support students in their out of class activities such as sport, music and drama. By doing that the students will know that you are interested in them and that you want them to do well. Their parents will appreciate your presence and will welcome the opportunity to talk with you.

Principals need the confidence of their school's community. That confidence is not easily given, but once given it is unlikely to be taken away. Most importantly, teachers will feel supported. If it is good enough for teachers to leave their families on a Saturday to coach a sports team, or in the evening to conduct a school choir, or hold a drama rehearsal, then the very least the principal can do is show up in support in order to 'know and care'. There is nothing more important in a principal's working day.

Principals are not allowed to have a 'bad hair day'. Predictability of mood is an essential characteristic of a good school leader. If people have to check on the mood of their leader before they make an approach, that leader has failed both themselves and those that they lead. However preoccupied a principal may be, there must always be time for a casual word of greeting or encouragement and time for those problems that may be of little significance in the principal's world, but in the world of a young teacher might be great. From time to time it is a useful exercise for a principal to reflect on past principals with whom they have worked. Perhaps our most effective role models are not those we most admire, but those from whom we have learned how best not to do our job. Think about things that principals did to you when you were a young teacher that made you feel uncomfortable or undervalued and make sure that you never do them now that you are the principal.

Leadership requires confidence in oneself as well as confidence in others. Leaders can contribute much to a school by ensuring that the best available people are appointed and given the best available resources to get on with the job. Teachers need their principals to give reasons for doing things. They do not need to be told why something should not be done. Good principals will recognize that when they encourage innovation and risk-taking they are also encouraging the development of a depth of leadership in their own school. One of the first things that must be realized is that while the principal might be the leader, the principal certainly is not the messiah. The vision principals need cannot be achieved by the charismatic efforts of a single individual. It will only be achieved through teamwork and through persuading others to share in it.

Principals who are leaders have vision and encourage others to take risks. The complementary test of a principal's leadership is the extent to which teachers are held accountable for their performance within schools. There has been a recognizable reluctance by principals to act quickly and decisively in matters of teacher performance. Perhaps this is a reflection of the principal as 'head' teacher tradition. Principals are not teachers. They have been, for it remains an essential prerequisite for principalship, but that ceased the day they became principal.

There is a delicate balance to be achieved between the interests of teachers, students and parents. Teachers cannot be supported 'right or wrong'. If the principal does not stand up for the interests of students, no one else will. Principals who fail to hold teachers accountable also turn their back on any claim to leadership and effectively deny their schools the opportunity to excel.

Principals will learn more about leadership from reading history and biography than they will ever learn from reading textbooks on management. Leadership is a very personal thing that calls on all of the individual's resources of wisdom, experience, patience and compassion. It requires flexibility, confidence and risk-taking. It can be lonely and yet the rewards can be exhilarating. Recall Martin Luther King's 'we shall overcome' speech to the civil rights marchers who had gathered in Washington from all over the United States in 1963. Martin Luther King was not a manager. He did not say, 'I have a plan'. He was a leader, he said, 'I have a dream'.

That is what every good principal should have – a dream!

2

An agenda for change

DAVID BENNETT

My own head teacher laughed when I told him during the one careers lesson that I had at school that I wanted to teach. For some reason I was not dissuaded. After graduating in mathematics and gaining a postgraduate Certificate of Education, I started my career in the fee-paying sector. My first appointments were in two boys' colleges, in the second of which I was head of department. A break from education followed with three years on the staff of a church in Hertfordshire, working mainly among young people. This time out was important because I was able to reflect on the role of education among young people from a totally different perspective. It was a particular challenge to consider what the service offered to all and not just the privileged few. I recommenced teaching in the late 1970s with a commitment to the state sector and comprehensive education. Two senior positions followed: the first in a multicultural college in West London, followed by the deputy headship of a large college in rural Essex. My first headship began in 1986 at Charles Darwin College, Biggin Hill, in the London borough of Bromley. The college was ready for development and many of the staff eagerly anticipated change under new leadership. In the first four years a new direction for Charles Darwin was established, before I branched out to make a contribution to the wider educational community through speaking engagements, consultancy and membership of the Secondary Heads Association (SHA) national council. At the same time I obtained an MBA at the Henley Management College.

After more than seven years it was time to move on to a fresh challenge. My agenda had been completed and Charles Darwin needed a new leader to implement the next stage of its development. I was appointed to the post of principal at Sackville Community College in January 1994. In addition to developing the work of the college, I have continued to play a national and international role through the work of SHA, the European Secondary Heads' Association (ESHA) and the International Confederation of Principals (ICP). In 1999 the Department of Education and Employment (DfEE) recruited me as a specialist adviser on college leadership and the international dimension in the professional development of teachers.

SACKVILLE COMMUNITY COLLEGE

THE SOCIO-ECONOMIC CONTEXT

Two hundred years ago carriages belonging to the English gentry changed horses at East Grinstead on their way from London to the coast at Eastbourne. It was also an ideal location for forays into Ashdown Forest, which at one time had covered much of southern England. As a result, this historic town about 50 kilometres south of London has long traditions that lay undisturbed for many years. The most significant changes in the town's history occurred during a period of 25 years after the Second World War. Gatwick, about 13 kilometres away, expanded to become a major international airport, the railway south of the town was closed and a rapid expansion of medium-size private housing took place. However, the failure to develop both the east–west and north–south road access, and railway closure to the south, constrained the attractiveness of the town for London commuters.

Today, East Grinstead is a pleasant place in which to live and work. Most parents work in the town or in the Gatwick employment area. Some commute to south and central London. Although a number work in the professions, most occupy support service positions and some are employed in manual work. Parents have high expectations of education, are supportive of the work of the colleges, but are largely content to leave the service to get on with its task. For example, 90 per cent attendance at a parents' consultation evening is the norm, but the parents' association struggles to gain support.

Education in West Sussex became fully comprehensive in the early 1970s. Two 11–18 secondary colleges serve the town, each with some 1500 students. Sackville serves the southern and eastern areas of East Grinstead, with 20 per cent of the intake coming from the surrounding villages in Surrey, Kent and East Sussex.

A COLLEGE PORTRAIT

Teachers find Sackville a comfortable place to work. The students are largely compliant and public examination results are well above the national average. East Grinstead and the surrounding district is a delightful area in which to live, work and bring up a family. Even Brighton and the south coast are within easy reach of the college for visits or residence. On taking up my appointment, I was therefore not surprised to discover that the staff turnover was quite low. Nearly half the teachers had started their career at the college and their average age was 43. Amongst my concerns was the discovery that, of the 30 middle or senior managers, only three were women, although two-thirds of the teachers were female. There appeared to be have been few major developments in the previous 25 years. Nor had the college been involved in any of the national initiatives that occurred during that period. In short, using the words of one of the vice-principals, 'the college had stagnated and had become complacent'.

Superficially all appeared to be successful. Sackville was popular with parents, the examination results were well above the national average, a full range of extra-curricular activities was on offer and parents liked the low staff turnover. Teachers relished the security of a pleasant area in which to live and were at ease with students who largely did not challenge them. Many staff had not changed their teaching material nor their approach for a number of years and they saw little need to do so. Some appreciated that the education service had developed elsewhere, but they were caught between their inexperience of effective change, their ignorance of how to manage a development, and the complacency of others who just wanted things to go on as they had always done.

Newly qualified staff were not so happy. They knew that things should be different, but were intimidated by the small number who favoured the *status quo*. There were few opportunities for internal promotion and most moved on after two or three years. Little attempt had been made to harness the enthusiasm of youth. The internal resistance to change was therefore significant, led by a small but powerful body whose mantra was 'If it ain't broke, don't fix it'. The problem was that many had been at Sackville for so long that they did not know how different things could and should be in order to provide the best for young adults of the 21st century. Most importantly, there had not been a will at leadership level to grapple with the challenges facing the college and to lead the change in culture that was so obviously necessary.

Externally matters were very different. Change was the norm. The radical Education Act of 1988 had heralded the first phase of a range of fundamental changes in English education. Information and communications technology (ICT) provided both a challenge and an effective learning tool. Young people were living in a culture that had already accepted change as the norm rather than the exception. Those who glimpsed the future realized that change was here to stay and the sooner the practices of effective change management were adopted, the more able the institution would be to harness the benefits for students.

Although Sackville had implemented the National Curriculum and received its own delegated budget, the main thrust of educational transformation occurring elsewhere had bypassed the college. On arrival I found only a handful of written policies, the development plan was a list of tasks to be undertaken, decisions were largely taken 'on the hoof', the curriculum planning group had 40 members and job descriptions were non-existent. Decision-making was largely autocratic as there were no procedures for effective consultation and consensus conclusions. Even the leadership team was viewed only as a sounding board for the principal. Governors and the local education authority knew that things had to change. Fortunately the perceptive members of staff knew that too. They were waiting for a lead, but they also knew that the few who wished to retain the *status quo* would resist vigorously.

SIGNIFICANT CHANGES

On taking up appointment it was clear that I would have to lead from the front. Such a stance would require careful planning in order to harness the enthusiasm of those who wished to move forward and to minimize the effect of resistance. Having spent the first term listening, during personal interviews with all members of staff and meetings for all groups of parents, and by using my eyes around the college, I was ready to seek the support of governors and to propose the way forward to staff.

Vision and values needed to be set in consultation with various parties, but teaching and learning were to be the key element of the reforms. A framework was needed to establish both the principles and the means of achieving them. A diagrammatic summary of the proposals is shown in Figure 2.1. The governing body and management structure were to play key roles in developing and implementing the policy respectively.

management structure

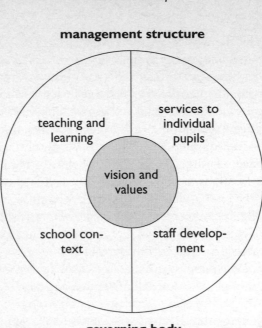

governing body

Figure 2.1 *The Sackville 2000 project*

In order to move the college forward, I proposed a number of key elements. These included:

- an extension of the teaching week from 23 hours 20 minutes to 25 hours;
- the design and implementation of a system of self-review and evaluation, which had classroom observation at its heart;
- the reorganization of the teaching staff into seven key teams, known as 'faculties';
- a structured college development plan that included team planning as an integral part of the whole;
- a focus on the importance of team leadership, with delegated authority but acting within a policy framework;
- a range of policies to provide a framework for improvement and development;
- use of the full range of learning opportunities offered by ICT and educational visits.

At heart there was a need to see the development of teaching and learning as the primary focus. Much of the plan's content had arisen from discussions with staff and parents. It was the principal's task to articulate possibilities and for the governors to consider the way forward. The first step was to take the ambitious plan to the governing body. Following their approval the project, known as 'Sackville 2000', was presented to staff together with a range of opportunities outlining how they could contribute to the development process. More than half the teaching staff subsequently volunteered to give additional time to such work. This represented a firm commitment to the agenda for change.

With the benefit of hindsight, I did not foresee that members of staff were experiencing an additional pressure. The previous *modus operandi* was for staff to be consulted on some decisions, but rarely did they participate in the decision-making process itself. The staff's view had been that the principal was appointed to lead the college. Whilst they needed to be consulted, he should make the decisions. Some complained about the result but most put their heads down and got on with the job of teaching. A trivial example encountered in my first term was that the principal was expected to approve every letter that was sent from the college, both before and after it was typed, and then to personally sign them! Members of staff were simply not used to taking responsibility. In the words of one colleague, 'the new principal was asking staff to move from a political style of decision-making, where those who shouted the loudest got their way, to one of consensus leadership where staff, particularly team leaders, were expected to carry responsibility for their own decisions'.

After gaining approval from the governors, the difficulty was knowing where to start. Much needed to be done. I knew that the major challenge when implementing change was to get the right balance between structure, process and focus. In my first headship at Charles Darwin I had mistakenly believed that if the structure was right everything else would follow. Such a stance delayed the effectiveness of the necessary changes. They did occur but they took longer. A primary concentration on structure can lead to an inflexible bureaucracy. On the other hand, seeking to implement a process of change in the absence of an appropriate framework to support and guide such action can result in confusion. In such a situation some staff fail to take action because they are uncertain about what is acceptable while others step into the vacuum and wield an independent authority. In addition, for changes to be effective in the key focus of teaching and learning, a strong group of curriculum team leaders would be needed. Without such support the leadership of the principal and vice-principals, however good it may have been, was likely to founder.

As a result, one major structural change without which it would have been impossible to achieve the primary focus, was necessary. All areas of the curriculum were combined into one of seven faculties. This necessitated the appointment of heads of faculty, some of whom already held posts at the college. The planning board of 40 members was scrapped and replaced by a board of studies comprising the heads of faculty and members of the college's leadership team. From the start it was made clear that this was to be the decision-making body in relation to teaching and learning. Although it took about a year to establish a different way of working, this body quickly developed its own identity. The members were eager to take on their new roles. They relished the opportunity to take increased responsibility and wanted to work as part of an effective team. The investment of time made to ensure that this body functioned appropriately has subsequently borne immense benefit. Although each member presents the views of his or her own team, it is now rare that consensus decisions are not reached. The board began its work within two months of the initial report.

To enhance this development, the principal and vice-principals retained the major responsibility for pedagogical leadership, thus ensuring that the critical nature of the key focus was led from the top. It also involved both vice-principals directly in the learning of students and the line management of the seven heads of faculty. Thus, each of the three most senior staff had their own coherent portfolio of work, but they shared the leadership of teaching and learning. I had long since held the view that to vest responsibility for curriculum leadership in one person was a mistake. Not only is the task too large for a single post, but all deputies need experience of this primary responsibility. The decision to share the role between the three most senior staff subsequently ensured that the driving force for change in teaching and learning remained, and continues to be at the top of the college's agenda.

Having established a structure for the oversight of teaching and learning, the other change processes were then put into practice. Working parties, each led by a senior member of staff, but none by the principal, commenced their work. Within six months the principal and board of studies developed a process for college development planning and a framework to review the work of the faculties. A programme of policy development was also implemented. In order to draw staff away from the mode of operation of my predecessor I led from the front throughout this stage whilst increasingly drawing staff into the process. Once the early principles and practices had been established, I changed my style of leadership to the rear in order to encourage staff and facilitate further developments.

MAIN PROBLEMS

The implementation of change is liked by few. Insecurity and opposition has a strange habit of appearing in the most unlikely places and at unexpected times. On the other hand, the experience of school improvement suggests that a discontinuity will eventually occur. Once it does, a second stage is necessary to secure improvement. Many schools that set their sights on improvement experi-ence initial discontinuity between the old and the new. Complaints arise about the necessity of change. Staff may leave and new practices are implemented. When such a discontinuity has occurred, the secret of a lasting improvement is to make sure that changes are followed through vigorously over a considerable period of time. Being confident in the justification for change, holding to the vision and seeing through its implementation are all vital elements if the desired improvement is to be accomplished.

I knew of the importance of these factors both from my own experience and that of others. The preparation, by listening to colleagues and parents, was effec-tive. Many of their ideas were included in Sackville 2000. The draft plans were discussed with the vice-principals and their comments further honed the propos-als. Finally, the plans were taken to the senior governors, the chair, vice-chair and the two committee chairs. They had already indicated that changes needed to occur. This had been in their mind when making the appointment of the new prin-cipal. They were offered a choice. The changes could be implemented over a 10-year period, or a much shorter timescale could be chosen. If it was the latter, there would be some opposition and the full support of the governing body would be needed to see the proposals through.

Conscious that 10 years would see almost two generations of students pass-ing through the college, the senior governors opted for the faster route. The full governing body subsequently welcomed the proposals and gave them their full support. The careful planning continued, with a full briefing of staff a few days later, followed by written details of how the proposals were to be implement-ed. A range of consultation exercises with staff took place over the following 12 months.

However, I had overlooked two important matters. Staff were not used to being involved in the decision-making process. They believed wrongly that there were hidden agendas and solutions had already been prepared. Whilst it was appropri-ate for me to specify non-negotiable elements at the outset, colleagues did not believe that the power for making decisions, or at least recommending action, on a range of details had been given to them. For example, the remit for the work-ing group on extending the college week clearly stated that it needed to be 25 hours rather than the previous 23 hours 20 minutes. Proposals for the curriculum balance and the structure of the teaching week were left to the group. New to such a responsibility, the working group finally refused to make a proposal and hand-ed it back for me to decide.

The leadership team urged me to retake the lead on this matter. However, I was still anxious to ensure that staff should contribute to the decision-making process and learn how to take such a significant responsibility. I delegated the task to the board of studies. Being a curriculum issue, it lay within their remit and the group comprised the most senior members of staff. In addition, it would be the heads of faculty, all members of the board, who would eventually be responsible for implementing the decision. They were finally faced with a choice between two options. The decision was reached on a majority vote, a consensus view having eluded them. Looking back, it is interesting to note that this was one of the few occasions when this newly emerging body took a vote. The board learnt from this experience and almost all its subsequent decisions have been on the basis of consensus.

The second factor that was overlooked was the need for the governors' decision to be outlined to parents at a formal meeting. They needed to hear directly of the plans, together with the justification, even though many of them were still at an embryonic stage. Whilst they were advised in writing, no face-to-face meeting took place. As it transpired, a small caucus of staff, that was finding the prospect of change difficult, used both of these loopholes. The uncertainty about the new nature of decision-making was exploited by the few to sow confusion amongst the many who wished to support change. For a period of time many staff were persuaded that there were other agendas, whereas I had in fact put my cards fully on the table. The majority of staff were caught in a triangle between the arguments of a few, the belief that forward was the only way to go and the natural desire to seek harmonious working relationships. Most of the small caucus had been at Sackville for a number of years and therefore knew many parents. Disquiet was fuelled among the latter group, which sadly burst into the public domain sometime later.

The uncertainty lasted for a period of about six months, though the fallout was longer. In order to mitigate the effect of this action, the vice-principals and I sought to persuade staff on an individual basis. In private, this proved to be an effective process, but only a few colleagues were brave enough to express openly their support at the height of the debate. Subsequently many staff and parents have admitted that they were wrong to oppose the changes. They have been gracious enough to accept that their own judgements were at fault and they had allowed themselves to be persuaded by the few. As a result of much work over a long period of time, the staff is a much more harmonious body today.

SACKVILLE COLLEGE TODAY

The appointment of two-thirds of the staff preceded my arrival, but they are now working in a very amicable series of teams. They eagerly embrace change and look for opportunities to take the initiative. Women hold one in three of the middle and senior posts. Even 50–50 is in sight. Staff development is at a significantly higher level than seven years previously and training is much more imaginative. For example, 12 members of staff have been involved in the piloting of international locations as part of their professional development. Almost all decisions are based on consensus, with the leadership team and board of studies being particularly effective in this regard.

The original developments in teaching and learning have all been implemented and others have continued to evolve. The self-review programme, now in its sixth year, is a standard feature of the college's professional work. Viewed with natural suspicion in its early days, all teachers now welcome the opportunity for a senior colleague to observe their lessons and to engage in the subsequent professional dialogue. Originally led by the principal and vice-principals, other members of the leadership team now also exercise this function. Most faculties have devised their own patterns for observation and support in order to help all teachers to enhance their teaching skills and thus develop the learning opportunities for students.

Members of staff with key responsibilities relish the freedom they have for decision-making within the overall policy framework. The change of focus in visits, from recreational to educational, has stimulated an ambitious range of activities, most of which are directly linked to the curriculum, with preparation and follow-up integral to the visit. Staff have themselves proposed and implemented many curriculum activities, such as the curriculum enhancement week when the timetable for 12- to 14-year-olds is suspended to allow for more extended activities. The 25-hour week has settled down, is liked by the majority of staff and students and is having an effect on the raising of achievement.

Above all, public examination results at both ages 16 and 18 have continued to improve over the last four years and are now well above the level before my arrival. Even more importantly, the college has seen a steady rise in the value-added indicators that measure the achievements of individual students against their prior level of attainment. At age 18 the results of all but one of the departments are now above the national average when individual results are compared to those of the same students at 16. A similar pattern has been achieved at 16 when comparison is made with prior attainment at 14. In addition, of the 40 secondary schools in West Sussex, Sackville has been in the top three on the value-added measures for the last two years, having risen from an average level of a few years ago. Such significant strides forward are directly attributable to the emphasis on teaching and learning over the last six years and to the ceaseless work of competent staff who have been committed to raising student achievement.

THE PRINCIPAL'S STYLE

Leadership is about ideas and inspirations, dreams and visions, aspirations and hopes. It is also about communicating the dream, persuading others of the validity of the cause and inspiring them to follow. Ultimately it focuses on the plans necessary to achieve the vision. In considering what style should predominate at any one time, three issues need to be addressed. The style needs to be fit for the purpose, fit for the personnel involved and fit for the context. Leadership operates at a range of levels. On the large scale, I had to lead from the front when first appointed, in order to draw the peripheral *ad hoc* decision-making back to the centre and to set the direction for the following years. The college's external inspection by the Office for Standards in Education (Ofsted), which occurred in 1996, confirmed that the change of style had already reaped its rewards. 'Strong leadership and management gives the college a clear sense of purpose and direction, focused on raising the standard of achievement and improving the quality of education for all students.'

After three years I deliberately changed my style to lead from the rear, encouraging others to take the lead and equipping them to do so. By that time team leaders knew what was expected of them, were confident of the college's direction and relished the opportunity to exercise a leadership role. They knew that I would always pick them up and encourage them if their plans did not succeed. Each team leader now has a mentor relationship with the principal or one of the vice-principals. This is often used to talk through ideas and aspirations before they are introduced and implemented.

Fitness for personnel is equally important. It is rare for a principal to have complete choice over staff appointments. The norm is for a group to be inherited. The staff at Charles Darwin College were ready for change. All that was needed was for them to be set in the right direction and to light the touch paper. Sackville was different. So too was the chosen style. After opting to lead from the front, the circle was gradually widened to those who could be trusted with tasks. All leaders when first in post need to identify those who are willing to move forward and take responsibility. It is not a question of looking for the 'yes' people. That course of action produces a series of clones, a disaster in any organization. The priority must be to identify those who are prepared to think and work in a creative and positive manner whilst supporting the achievement of the vision.

My style has always been to work with and through colleagues. People are the best resource in any organization. But unless their work is harnessed and fashioned to meet the core purpose and vision, there is little that principals can do on their own. Whilst leading from the front, I chose to develop colleagues in the first three years in order to release their potential to move forward at an even faster pace.

The third strand is fitness for context. Newly appointed principals have to build upon the decision-making styles of their predecessors. I was quite prepared to take decisions on my own, but a move to a consensus and collaborative approach was essential. This could not be achieved overnight. In the beginning there had to be a degree of autocracy, but decisions were always talked through with the vice-principals. Development of a consensus and collaborative style had to start with them, but it takes time to develop. Over a period of three years, which was longer than had first been hoped, the culture changed slowly from autocracy to the desired style of consensus. At times this required a firm, some would say inflexible, stance on a range of issues, but the style eventually produced the desired impact. Whichever approach is adopted, ultimately effective leadership is not a question of style but of impact.

The consultative approach increasingly bore fruit, so that after six years the college itself has adopted the same style in a range of decision-making areas. The leadership team now provides a strong and effective corporate leadership for the whole college. Staff know that whoever they ask on the team, they will get a similar answer. After six years, I rarely made a major decision without consulting the vice-principal or the leadership team. This is done not because I lack the courage or will. I know that my own views need to be honed, there needs to be a wider base for decision-taking and because I wish to involve senior colleagues in the college's leadership. I am also aware that those whom I lead will weigh my commitment to openness, honesty, professional integrity and a passion for fairness. After all, one of them will be sitting in my seat one day.

Shortly after my appointment I decided upon 12 cultural changes that I considered would encapsulate the extent to which the planned changes had been effective. These were shared with the vice-principals after six months and with the remainder of the senior leadership team a year later. Four years was my original target for achieving the change of culture, but it took six. Most targets have been achieved fully and the remainder in part, but six years is a fitting reminder that achieving a change in culture is a long, and sometimes laborious, process. It does not happen overnight, nor even in 12 months, and it might take six years!

Data, ethos and gender: the improvement jigsaw

CHRIS NICHOLLS

I had always anticipated that I might become a teacher. Coming from a working-class background and benefiting, as did many of my contemporaries, from a grammar school education, I recognized from an early age that success at school was the key to improving my own life chances. I perceived teaching as a high-status profession and it was one to which I could aspire. I admired many of those who taught me.

My choice of sciences at A-Level was more to do with competence than interest and that of the University of London very much the opportunity to break away from the small Somerset town in which I grew up.

A notice displayed in the student union bar, an appeal for volunteer help, led to my first direct experience of the classroom in a local East End primary school. Here I encountered for the first time the real difficulties that disadvantaged youngsters from a multitude of backgrounds face and the challenge this presents to their teachers. I was willing but hopelessly inadequate. To this day I remember the head teacher whose patience and authority permeated the school. I first met him with a small, recently arrived Biafran child in tow who had already recognized, despite the fact that he understood no English, that this was a man he could trust. He was remarkable, a natural leader, which was obvious to all who worked for him long before performance indicators or competences had been invented.

Having decided to delay a career decision by continuing at university to tackle a PhD, I was persuaded to accept a part-time post teaching chemistry. This was in a large secondary school undergoing the transformation from a selective grammar into a mixed co-educational comprehensive. On the one day a week I was given the task of teaching eight successive lessons to Year 9 students who spanned the ability and attitude range, but for whom there appeared to be a common work scheme and resources. Again I found myself unprepared and unable to meet the challenge. I did not continue past my first year. This was the point at which I decided that I did not have the skills to become a teacher!

I joined the Inland Revenue on its accelerated promotion scheme and soon found myself with an office, two telephones, a secretary and second only to the district inspector in terms of my authority. It was incredibly boring. To my surprise I began to appreciate that files, facts and figures were much less interesting than people and I knew that I had to make a change. By contrast, many of my peers at university, with whom I was in regular contact, had completed their Post Graduate Certificate in Education (PGCE), were beyond their probationary years and talked excitedly about their jobs and prospects. I began to think again about joining them, but it was a major decision to give up the exalted position I had already reached to become a classroom teacher. To this day it is a decision I have never regretted.

My opportunity arrived when a vacancy arose in a local girls' grammar school, itself destined to become a co-educational comprehensive within two years. Here was a chance to learn the craft of the classroom in a very protected environment. The PGCE was tackled in evening classes, though obtaining the certificate was not a requirement at the time. Despite my earlier experiences, I wanted, even at that stage, to become a head teacher. I have always been ambitious, I had given up a senior management position with significant prospects and I felt I owed it to myself.

My career was not planned with military precision, though I did set myself targets and the position into which I had fallen was ideal. Within a year I was 'in charge' of physics, a year head shortly after and 'senior' year head within five years. The school, in an outer London borough, was struggling to cope with its new comprehensive status, but I seemed to be developing strategies to cope with youngsters of all types. I was thriving and, much more importantly, enjoying every minute of it. My own education had brought me into contact with children from affluent backgrounds and professional parents, but the boys with whom I had grown up were the sons of factory workers, farm labourers and dockers and I was at ease with them. My first experiences of inner-London schools had been a real culture shock, but I was beginning to meet the challenge of the comprehensive school.

I was promoted four times in my first school and needed to move on. In 1982 I joined my present school, Moulsham High in Essex, as a senior teacher, deputy head of upper school. Eighteen months later I became its deputy head. I was 32 and had just seven years' teaching experience behind me. At the time I would not have imagined becoming head teacher in the same school, but equally well could not have anticipated the changes in school management that 1988 would bring. By then, my predecessor's retirement was on the horizon and, although he was enthusiastic about the local management of schools, at this late stage in his career he did not need to become conversant with the detail of personnel law and budgets. He was a man passionately interested in the education of children, their curriculum and in ensuring their good behaviour. It was both appropriate and hugely advantageous that I should learn the new skills.

I was able to forge a relationship with the governing body, which was somewhat unusual for a deputy head in 1990. Despite the fact that Moulsham High School was large with 1250 students, had a sound reputation and would therefore be seen as ideal for 'second headship', I knew that my application would be considered seriously and decided to wait for the opportunity. I was appointed head teacher in January 1991.

MOULSHAM HIGH SCHOOL

The school was formed in 1973 by the amalgamation of two county secondary schools, one for boys and one for girls. It is situated in Chelmsford, the county town of Essex, and is currently one of 10 secondary schools in that town. The characteristics of its immediate catchment have not changed significantly since its formation and the majority of children come from owner-occupied homes, though not necessarily affluent ones. The percentage of children known to be eligible for free school meals is below the national average, as is the number with statements of special educational need. Somewhat surprisingly there is a larger number of pupils speaking English as an additional language than is normal for a school of this type.

In most respects Moulsham is like many county 11–18 co-educational comprehensives, though the presence of two highly selective grammar schools in the town does have a marginal impact. In one respect, however, it is unique. Since its formation, a policy of single-sex education within a mixed school has been pursued. Boys and girls have always been taught separately between the ages of 11 and 14 (Key Stage 3) and for the core subjects in the following two years (Key Stage 4). They are mixed for their options and for all post-16 provision. All social activities and areas are fully integrated. This was the organization to which I came in 1982 and which I inherited as head teacher in 1991.

From my earliest days in the school I was struck by how little this organization appeared to impact upon the teachers who worked in it. It was accepted, relatively popular, but there was no obvious data available to determine its impact, either academic or social. Pedagogic advice for those who might wish to meet the challenge of teaching boys and girls separately did not appear to be available. To some extent this remains the case today.

In the mid-1980s the reputation of the school was strong in the local community, but I think it fair to say that we were at odds with mainstream educational thinking. The gender issue made us different, but streaming and setting, assertive behavioural policies and a strong emphasis on traditional teaching were, to say the least, unfashionable.

An inspection by HMI in 1986 concluded: 'The school is an orderly, hardworking community with a competent and professional staff guiding responsible and responsive pupils who achieve satisfactory standards of work.' Concerning the single-sex organization they were ambivalent. There appeared to be some advantages, though insufficient evidence was available to sustain the view that it was universally beneficial. At the onset of headship I was well aware that this type of organization was in real need of evaluation, and possibly review.

Throughout the 1980s in Chelmsford, like many similar towns, the demographic trend had led to a significant surplus of school places. The local education authority had been managing this problem by amending catchment areas and Moulsham's roll had been reduced from 1700 to 1250 by the time I became head teacher. The planned further reduction to 1000 had been halted by the introduction of parental choice in 1988. A small number of parents from outside the catchment area were opting for the school and this compensated for those who were transferred to the grammar schools or chose a Catholic education.

Parental choice in Chelmsford was very real. A relatively small geographical area contained a number of secondary schools offering quite diverse provision and all heads were wary of competition for places. Marketing policies emerged and co-operation and collegiality became more difficult. Moulsham was under no immediate threat, but other schools were working hard to ensure their futures. Our continuing popularity was an item that constantly re-emerged in senior management team discussions.

ON TAKING UP HEADSHIP

Becoming head teacher of a school that you know well is a mixed blessing. I think my appointment was relatively popular with staff, though this was more to do with a feeling of ensured continuity than any personal characteristics. Staff felt secure. They liked the school the way that it was. They were aware of the fact that we were different from many other schools and they were fearful of radical change. In a way this set my agenda very clearly. I needed to retain the ethos and, in particular, the very high standards of behaviour. However, I was unsure how well we were performing and was unclear as to the benefits, or otherwise, of our separate gender organization. We felt we were a good school, but we had no real evidence. We had also become isolated from our community, particularly from the education authority that was supposed to support us. We sensed that they disapproved of the way that we did things and we felt undervalued. One's tendency in such circumstances is to become introspective. I needed to resolve these difficulties without compromising our position.

Moulsham High School never did develop a marketing strategy. Instead we focused our attentions on raising standards, confident that parents could look beyond the brochure and the open evening. I have had no reason to change this view.

It is a common phenomenon for most head teachers to review management structures within the first two years of appointment. Whilst the publicly stated reasons will be efficiency, value and improved communication, there is clearly a sub-text that amounts to stamping one's personal authority on an institution. It can be argued that I was no different.

Of the three deputy head posts only one, in my view, offered a real platform for future headship. This was the position I had vacated and for which I was able to appoint a successor. Such was the nature of the other job descriptions, logistical, heavy workload and routine, that they did not allow for a real contribution to strategic leadership. Leadership is a collegiate activity. It is essential that more than one individual has the time and opportunity to reflect upon the institution's needs and to consider its future direction. I would have addressed this issue immediately, but one of the incumbents had been appointed by my predecessor and was recently in post. It seemed unreasonable to change so soon the nature of the job for which he had applied.

I waited two years, during which time I could see the school's roll beginning to grow, and was then able to make a number of changes which I felt to be in the school's interest. This organization is largely in place today and it has served the school well, but its great strengths are also its weaknesses. I succeeded in creating a small, but highly effective, strategic senior management team and I have appointed five deputy heads in ten years. Its membership has changed many times. This constant renewal has been hugely beneficial to me personally and to the school as a whole.

The school is divided into three sections – lower, middle and upper – each led by a team of three. These are the people with whom pupils and parents have most contact. Such an organization allows for the creation of a small-school atmosphere within a large school and makes students feel more secure. The pastoral system is enormously strong and teachers welcome the immediacy of support that they receive from heads of school.

The three senior teachers who lead the school sections have substantial devolved responsibility. They are key figures. The demands of their task are such, however, that they do not have a significant opportunity to influence the strategic development of the school as a whole. The same can be said of the powerful and well-structured departmental leadership, which also has senior teachers amongst its number. The system is focused and efficient. People know what their task is and they perform it well. The school runs smoothly and communication is good. Careful thought would have to be given before changing or abandoning such arrangements.

The fact has to be faced, however, that the senior teachers sometimes feel more like middle management than leaders. This is a problem with which I continue to struggle. Knowing where you want to go only solves half of the problem. You need to know where you are. This applies to the development of an institution and also to those who work in it. I remember quite vividly addressing my colleagues in my first year of headship and asking that each head of department make an appointment with me to discuss performance. Given that we knew each other very well, I do not think that this announcement caused undue alarm, though in the event subject leaders were ill-prepared.

USING AVAILABLE DATA

A systematic review of current and historical data, including our expectations for the future, was not anticipated, nor were questions involving the performance of individual classes and, by inference, teachers. The meetings were neither confrontational nor accusatory, but there was a healthy discussion about the facts as we perceived them. A climate of accountability began to be established. I have never doubted the quality or professionalism of the people with whom I have worked and I have rarely felt the need to direct a particular course of action or spell out a weakness. Rather, colleagues have been engaged in review of the best available data and have then been allowed to set their own targets. With each passing year subject leaders have improved their understanding of departmental performance. They approach review meetings as prepared as I am and often with additional data and information. These meetings now include deputy heads of department and deputy head mentors.

The sophistication of the information available to us today far exceeds the relatively crude examination statistics that were used in the early 1990s. The systems we have developed allow for an analysis of performance using 'added value' methodology by subject, by gender and by ability. I am totally aware of the unreliability of statistics and I have encouraged a healthy scepticism, but the underlying aim is clear. We must use the data to improve our own performance and not to compare ourselves with others. Even now, 10 years on, not all staff are comfortable with the use of data, but we have come a long way.

We have taken similar approaches with students. The procedures have taken many years to develop. We started using added value and target setting processes long before they were in vogue. Individual interviews carried out by senior, well-trained staff using a wealth of information, but particularly a mechanism which tracks progress through school, allow all pupils to set their own targets annually. Young people enjoy talking about themselves and, in the main, are well able to analyse their strengths and weaknesses. They set themselves appropriate goals and we have been able to analyse the success of this for a number of years. We are convinced that it has contributed to the improvements that we have seen.

The skill of the interviewer is paramount in all of this. Data handled badly achieves little and often causes harm. Imposed targets are of little use unless they are accompanied by threat, which is in itself damaging. However, those set by an individual from a common understanding can be very powerful. We know that the improvement in targeted grades is twice that of the improvement in others.

The gender issue has been, and remains, an enormous challenge. I now know what we are achieving and, whatever my initial perceptions, would be extremely reluctant to change our existing organization. Boys and girls do perform differently at Moulsham, as they do in the nation as a whole, but the rates of improvement are the same for both sexes and substantially above those of their counterparts nationally.

Here my message has been 'if we are to organize this way then let us exploit it', but this has been difficult to convey. Even raising awareness of the issue is problematic. Intrinsically, staff want to treat people equally. Encouraging them to consider varying their teaching styles, learning organizations, resources or assessment methodologies to accommodate the preferences of boys or girls is not easy. It is clear, however, that the atmosphere and interaction in boys' and girls' classes is different. In most cases this does not arise from a deliberate strategy, but from good teachers adapting to the circumstances in which they find themselves.

The behavioural challenge, particularly of boys of below average ability, remains with us, but it is precisely these groups with whom we must succeed if we are to maintain our current levels of performance and improve further. In my view, maintaining a civilized atmosphere underpins everything. Without good behaviour, learning is inhibited. I am confident that we have succeeded in this. All those who visit the school tell me so, but I always fear complacency.

That the school has improved is beyond doubt, though I sometimes find it difficult to define precisely what part I have played. If I have done nothing else, I have managed to convince governors, parents, staff and students alike that we are an achieving school. The climate of expectation is high and this is surely important. GCSE results have increased from 3 per cent to nearly 20 per cent above national norms and this during a period when the ability of the intake has declined. The roll has risen from 1250 to 1600 and the school is now full with a substantial waiting list. There has been a healthy turnover of staff, with the vast majority leaving for promotion. Our foreign visits and student exchanges have extended beyond Europe to Africa and China and the reputation of the school is spreading outside the immediate locality. It would be fair to say that in some respects we are perceived as innovative and at the forefront of development. The school has experienced media interest both locally and nationally. In some aspects, however, it retains its traditional feel and may be all the better for it.

SOME THOUGHTS ON SCHOOL LEADERSHIP

I am a head teacher and, by definition, a school leader. As such, I am inundated by government initiatives, the demand for change and for raising standards. I am accountable to almost everybody and acutely aware that the interests of staff, students, parents, the community, governors and government all have to be served. It is perhaps unfortunate that their interests are not always the same. That which improves the chances of students, or leads to 'better value', may worsen the conditions under which teachers work. It is something of a juggling act.

Like all good jugglers, I know that my task becomes more complex as I increase the number of balls in the air. It is also certain that occasionally one is going to hit the floor. Knowing that I am going to make mistakes and that I can do this without losing my credibility is important. I suspect that all leaders need that quiet confidence in themselves and in their capabilities, which allows them to put their errors into perspective. Having a real sense of perspective is important.

Devotees of the American cartoon character 'Charlie Brown' may recognize these rather wise words, which I had on my desk for many years: 'There is no problem too big or complicated in life that cannot be run away from.' Well, perhaps we may have to exchange 'run away' for 'resolved with calm, collective consideration' or even 'will not seem important in a relatively short space of time', but I suspect that too many head teachers suffer because they are too self-critical, perfectionist and unable to put things into proportion. Neither do I believe necessarily that that confidence which is so essential to 'living with one's mistakes' is something with which one is born. It comes from rational analysis and the recognition that the majority of one's decisions lead to successful outcomes and that people seem happy either with what you are or what you do.

Earlier I intimated that maintaining the school's ethos was, for me, a priority when I became head teacher. I am not sure that it translates to leadership in the widest context, but school leaders are clearly required to set the moral tone and espouse a set of values. This can be extraordinarily difficult because there are many more shades of grey in our modern, complex society than we would like, but this simply makes it even more important. School leaders must both set and exemplify this set of values if they are to prepare young people successfully for adult life.

The best in-service training that I have received and enjoyed has been that which has allowed the opportunity to share good practice with other school leaders. I am fascinated by the different ways in which people have sought to improve their schools. It is self-evident that very different people have achieved success with very different skills in many different ways and I am cautious of the blueprint. I am especially cautious of the competence-based approach that is currently prevalent. The process of defining the irreducible elements that define a good manager or good leader is a useful theoretical exercise, but there is an obvious danger. The logical extension, that people without these qualities could not possibly lead or manage well, flies in the face of observation. We know that there are good teachers whose organization and paperwork is poor. We also know that there are good leaders who lack the charisma that we deem to be so important.

Drawing the distinction between leadership and management has, I suspect, been a valuable exercise. It is clear that schools need good managers and good leaders, though I believe in the main that these should be the same people. Leadership is an enticing concept. It sounds authoritative, worthy and enormously important, though it is too easy to believe that it is the province of individuals.

Management, on the other hand, can sound logistical and functional, even manipulative and machiavellian, but we have never doubted that it was a team activity. We invented senior management teams and middle managers before leadership teams and curriculum leaders.

The best leadership comes when a small group of people, sharing a similar set of values and goals, are able to challenge each other constantly and do so, sure of their place in the team and confident of their equal value. In such an atmosphere, when the final decision does fall to one individual, it will be well supported. We must never forget that leadership is required at all levels in any institution.

The overwhelming evidence that good schools have good leaders cannot be ignored, but I worry about the notion of the 'charismatic head' without whom all would fail and who is seen as almost synonymous with the school. Leaders must manage change and this is a complex process, from idea generation, through refinement, consultation, decision-making and implementation, to evaluation. This is the province of many and no single part of it belongs to a particular set of people. Good ideas come from everywhere and the best institutions will recognize this. Whilst it can be advantageous to have a team made up of different people with different skills that are complementary, the greatest success will arise when team members understand all parts of the process and can contribute, challenge and question at any stage.

If we fear that a school will deteriorate because its head teacher has left, then we must conclude that an incomplete job has been done. Surely the best leaders are enablers. They will have developed not only the skills and competences of those they lead, but they will have given them the confidence that allows them to make their own decisions without fear. Real delegation is central to this process, as is ensuring that time is available for reflective thought. The notion I find much more attractive is that of the leader who is able to withdraw gradually, confident that others will not only manage, but might also innovate in the head's absence.

Really good head teachers are unreasonably optimistic. They believe in the enormous potential of people, particularly the young, to improve and to succeed. They have to be good at playing a part, but optimism is difficult to display when it is not genuinely felt. It is infectious and, when others are feeling stretched and depressed, it becomes even more essential that there is a collective belief that it will be 'all right in the end'. I doubt those who assert that their institutions have improved as much as they can and that they have already extracted every ounce that is possible. As a school, I know that Moulsham has done well and I know that the staff work long hours, but I see potential everywhere and remain ambitious for staff and students alike.

Whatever else they do, leaders must bring a sense of purpose and direction. 'Vision' is the word often used. It is a very powerful word and for me contains the notion of insight not given to many. I think we make a mistake, however, if this leads us to the conclusion that leaders are born, not made. Vision is rarely acquired on the road to Damascus. I did not enter teaching knowing what good schools were or what was good teaching or how it can be achieved. There have been very few occasions when a revelation has been so blindingly obvious that it has changed the course of my life. If I have achieved a sense of direction and purpose and the deep inner convictions that go with it, they have been gained by other means.

Direction and purpose can be derived from the accumulative experience of any professional's career. They come from learning to see things in their proper context; recognizing the place of the mundane in the bigger picture; anticipating what will come from that which has already passed and an endless thirst for continued learning. Good leaders never stop listening, they never stop thinking and they recognize that their own beliefs, however strongly felt, must hold up to rational analysis. Ultimately, they need to remember that they might be wrong.

4

A belief in multi-age

CHRIS PLANT

I began my teaching career in Brisbane, the capital of Queensland, the sub-tropical state of Australia, in the mid-1970s. My post lasted just six months before I was sent to a country school on the Darling Downs, the centre of Queensland's grain-growing industry. After a further three months I was transferred again to a north-western border town, with an aboriginal reserve, named Camooweal. This was my first introduction to teaching more than one grade in a single class and it would have a significant impact on my career. I was given a mixed-grade class of 20 students, mostly aboriginal. I remained for two years, experiencing the teaching of all primary grades in a co-operative teaching situation with another teacher.

My next appointment was back in Brisbane. After a year with a class of 12-year-olds, I applied to go to a small country school as a principal. Over time, I have been principal in nine different schools, one of them some 1600 kilometres north of Brisbane. With each new appointment the schools became progressively larger. This was the most common method of promotion and provided a sequential development of skills. A teacher was eligible for advancement after three years in a particular level of school. Today, the methodology is different with a public service merit model being employed, allowing individuals to jump levels and to come into principalship from diverse backgrounds.

MULTI-AGE

Many of the smaller schools were forced to have multiple grades within the single class. My first principalship was a one-teacher school in which there were seven grades and 16 students. The expectation at the time was that you must cover the full curriculum for the year, which necessitated separate curriculum planning for all grade levels. There was no significant acknowledgement that 'multi-age' meant planning strategies to emphasize common learning, grouping strategies, peer learning and integration. At the time, I longed to be in a single class, believing that life in general would be easier, with less planning and catering for narrower ability levels.

Multi-age comprises a number of grades working together in an integrated manner in one class and incorporates learning strategies that provide improved outcomes for all the students. As I progressed through different schools as a principal, I also maintained a programme of formal academic study and took the opportunity to study multi-age. This research later provided the basis for educational reform in a number of schools.

LEADERSHIP

Working in various schools, I was exposed to a variety of communities that included farming, country town and low socio-economic. I averaged three years per school until my last two. I have led these each for six years. The significant changes occurring in the last two schools have resulted from my commitment to multi-age. My leadership styles have changed as I have gained insights and experience. Added to this I have undertaken academic study, particularly in the field of school administration.

Accommodating a wide range of communities, all different, has tested my leadership. Each situation has required a different approach. In one community there was a belief that the local school principal should undertake certain leadership roles within the local community. In another, leadership outside the school was not encouraged. In each situation it was necessary to identify the community expectations and norms and to work within that context. However, my personal leadership traits remained consistent.

Principals who are not given the opportunity to interact within a number of diverse communities will not be able to temper their leadership skills through practice in diversity. Such experiences can be humbling as well as exhilarating. Some are career changing.

In 1994 I became the founding president of the Multi-age Association of Queensland. The association currently has 800 members in the state, other states and internationally. Being president has helped me in the change process that I have undertaken in my last two schools, particularly with respect to personal influence.

MUSGRAVE HILL SCHOOL

SOCIO-ECONOMIC CONTEXT OF THE SCHOOL

Musgrave Hill state school is on the Gold Coast of Queensland in the township of Southport. It is a complex school with over 80 staff and includes:

- a pre-school unit of 100 students aged 5;
- a primary unit of 400 students aged from 6 to 12 (Grades 1–7);
- a special education class of 22 students aged from 6 to 12;
- a special education development unit of 60 students from birth to 6 years old;
- an educational support service of 13 special education teachers that supports other schools.

The school has a significant low socio-economic level and was one of only four schools on the Gold Coast to attract federal funding to compensate for community needs. It has the usual characteristics found in such schools: a high transient rate; single-parent homes; low literacy and numeracy levels; significant behavioural and psychological problems and a reluctance of the parent community to engage with the school in a positive manner.

Of late, there has been a change of socio-economic background within junior classes. A number of parents now come from the middle classes, deciding to go to this school because of its alternative curriculum and classroom organization. How to cater for differences in culture within the same classroom and the cultural clashes that inevitably result is an emerging problem.

THE JOURNEY

The most significant innovation over the last six years of my leadership has been the change from a graded school to multi-age in both philosophy and practice. The school has passed through three distinct phases in establishing this innovation:

Phase 1   Preparing the school and community for the change: 'On arrival'.
Phase 2   Implementing the change: 'The formative years'.
Phase 3   Stabilizing the change: 'The establishing years'.

On arrival: 1994–95

On arriving at Musgrave Hill in July 1994 I found the school was losing students and there was a belief that it might be closed or become part of the neighbouring special school. The parent support group, the Parents and Citizens Association, was extremely positive and proactive in supporting the school. These parents had children in the senior section and were the remnants of the middle-class presence. The school had a proud history with numbers once in the 900s and was strategically positioned to accommodate the fast-growing new estates that were developing nearby.

Many of the teachers had been in the school for 20 years. A number had never taught in any other school. They were aware of the movement in the clientele and bemoaned the fact that students and parents had changed. Students now displayed less respect for their teachers and were more difficult to teach than a few years before.

The previous deputy principal had worked towards developing increased flexibility in the junior section and one multi-age class was in operation with a single teacher. Staff were aware of my multi-age bias due to my position in the newly formed Multi-age Association of Queensland. The issue was addressed at an early staff meeting. They were told that I would not force anyone into a multi-age setting and they would be given the choice. The practice was considered by many to be an unworkable model requiring them to spend long hours in planning without any advantages for the students. Much of this belief resulted from schools operating composite classes where two or three grades were put together. Teachers expected to cover all year programmes, just as would be expected for a single year level. This does require extra work and is complex. Teachers feel that the full curriculum expectations cannot be fulfilled. Composite grading is difficult and in most cases unworkable with Queensland class numbers.

Student behaviour and staff morale were the two top issues. Since I had come from a school with a low socio-economic background, I had experience in supporting communities with these problems. Whole staff meetings were used to discuss issues and ideas. The changes to behaviour policy were agreed, put into place and regularly reflected upon by the whole staff. This process allowed me to establish my credibility as a leader and communicator. Student behaviour became more effectively managed and staff morale improved.

External influences

In my first years at Musgrave Hill the Labour Government was in power in Queensland and was undertaking a reform called 'devolution'. At the time, other states had embraced school-based management. Devolution was Queensland's answer to the nationwide move.

Schools were asked to take on responsibilities that had previously been the preserve of the regional office. School offices were expected to carry the weight of these changes, but classroom teachers were generally unaware of the implications. Teaching methods remained unchanged. Devolution was a management rather than a curriculum change, although the authors in the education department argued that giving schools greater flexibility with their funds should improve educational outcomes.

At this time, Queensland's education department was undertaking a review entitled 'Focus on Schools'. Part of the review was the flexibility in infant years and beyond. I was involved in the working party to develop recommendations to be taken to senior management for endorsement. The advice to the working party was that the recommendations should be cost neutral. The changes, if accepted, had to be accommodated within the existing budget. As a result, the recommendations, needless to say, were insignificant. They had absolutely no impact on the system and were subsequently buried. Multi-age in senior executive circles of the department was not popular.

The change

That was the backdrop to the change process that was about to occur at Musgrave Hill. Initially, I had not intended to change the school to a multi-age. In the early years I was simply opportunist and used staff and situations to promote circumstances that were more conducive to multi-age. For example, when a staff member was transferred or left the school, I intentionally recruited someone more sympathetic to the process. Staff were placed in areas where I knew that their impact would make a difference to the school's philosophy. The term 'multi-age' was dropped in favour of 'flexibility'. I sensed that this would be more palatable to teachers and did not necessarily mean 'multi-age'. Change developed as a response to my own beliefs and their impact on the organization of the school.

As the years progressed, more and more classes became multi-age. In 1997 all the junior school Grades 1, 2 and 3 were multi-age. By 1999 the whole school had adopted the practice. It had also taken on a new innovation in multi-age, known as 'staging'.

'The formative years': 1996–98

At the beginning of 1996, a deputy principal was appointed to the school, allowing me to concentrate on the development of strategies to enhance flexibility in the classroom. We constructed a school mission statement highlighting the individual difference of students. Attached to this was a school charter, a powerful document that was used to promote the distinctiveness of the school. It was constantly referred to at staff meetings, in newsletters and in individual interactions. By establishing a commitment to individual difference, staff accepted multi-age more easily. It was justified by the need to teach according to the differences present in each child. For change to be successful there must be a common basis of understanding and a strong philosophical underpinning in order to provide resilience in times of threat.

External influences

During these years, a political change occurred. The Conservative coalition Government was voted into power. One result was a more intense move towards school-based management. Many principals found that their curriculum leadership expertise was being eroded. More and more of their time was consumed with budget and human resource issues. Their perception was that principals were being required to be managers rather than educational leaders. Primary school principals were proud of their tradition and the fact that they never lost touch with classroom practice. This development signalled a challenge to the tradition and resulted in significant conflict, both within the system and between schools.

The then director general of education, Frank Peach, introduced a school-based management scheme known as 'Leading Schools'. One third of large primary and secondary schools could apply for Leading School status. The carrot was extra funding for taking on extra responsibility with a more intensive competitive thrust. The Queensland teachers' union went on the attack and did not support the programme, saying it was unjust and not inclusive. School principals and their staff were at times in conflict. The department of education encouraged principals to participate in the programme despite the wishes of their staff.

After a year of conflict, schools settled into the Leading Schools programme. However, it was short-lived. Another change of government occurred. Labour was once again in control and shelved the programme. They replaced it with three options of school-based management from which a choice could be made.

Such systemic turmoil made curriculum innovation, such as multi-age, difficult because of the external agendas that were driving education. However, Frank Peach did set out his vision in his 'Schooling 2001' document:

20th century   ⟶   21st century

grade level, lock-step   ungraded, continuous progress,
approaches   team teaching

This position was used to further promote support at the school level for multi-age classes. External pressures were forcing the Musgrave Hill community to look at ways in which it was different and how, as a leading school, it might re-invent itself. This environment enabled greater acceptance of flexibility within classroom organization.

Strategies for change

After the first two years it became clear that the number of staff interested in taking a multi-age class was increasing. As older staff left and new staff arrived, the opportunity was taken to extend the process in the junior school. The breakthrough came when senior teachers, Grades 6 and 7, agreed to put students together in single multi-age classes. They agreed on the basis that this strategy would reduce behavioural problems in the senior school. Grade 7 students in a single class in their last year in primary school tended to misbehave more than other grade levels. Placing a Grade 6 group in this setting reduced the negative behaviours of the Grade 7 students. After the first year the teachers chose to continue with the arrangement.

To provide leadership in this area I used group decision-making strategies to obtain consensual agreement in order to undertake the change. During the year the teachers were provided with opportunities to discuss the strategy and modify practice where necessary.

At this point, the community was not directly involved in the change process. Information was provided at the regular community meetings such as parent nights and at the Parents and Citizens Association committee meetings. Because the decision by the senior teachers was more a reaction to student behaviour, it was not seen as a whole-school change to multi-age. Parents were generally accepting and agreed to almost any strategy if it would result in improved student behaviour.

At the same time, more classroom space became available and the trade-off for having multi-age classes was to give each teacher a double teaching space for a single class. This was possible due to falling rolls. Student behaviour also improved because of the increased space.

1998: the year of decision

Early in 1998 Mike Middleton, an educational networker, spoke at the annual general meeting of the Multi-age Association. Mike presented an approach that placed students in three stages instead of the traditional seven graded years. At the same time, the Queensland Education Department was developing its syllabus in levels and there were three for primary schools. Musgrave Hill was almost fully multi-age, but needed a defensible reason to embrace it fully. Stage- based learning, as espoused by Mike Middleton, proved to be the clear, logical argument to complete the change process.

During 1998 Mike Middleton was employed to undertake an intervention programme helping provide direction for staff undertaking the changes necessary to move to a stage-based school. The process included:

* meeting with administrators and teachers to identify where the school was on its journey;
* undertaking intensive planning sessions with small groups of teachers identified for their leadership abilities and their expected contribution to the school the following year;
* meeting with parents to provide information about stage-based learning;
* a staff meeting, without Mike Middleton, to formulate our own curriculum directions, emphasizing outcomes-based learning;
* the development of programmes for the coming year to give teachers confidence in the change.

Leadership at this stage involved participation in all meetings in order to explain the process to staff. Providing the vision and arousing enthusiasm was integrated into all interpersonal situations, whether group or individual, as well as promoting the process through the school newsletters, district meetings and conferences. The deputy principal was an integral part of this process. Her leadership and management of the curriculum enabled the change to be successfully accomplished. The curriculum was changed from a process emphasis to an outcomes-based model. This was a paradigm shift for many staff.

'The establishing years': the current situation

This started at the beginning of 1999 with all classrooms multi-age and within stages:

- Stage 1: Grades 1, 2 and 3 referred to as 'Junior Stage'.
- Stage 2: Grades 4 and 5 referred to as 'Middle Stage'.
- Stage 3: Grades 6 and 7 referred to as 'Senior Stage'.

Grade level names were disbanded in favour of colour, animal and surf beaches. For example: Junior Blue, Middle Platypus and Senior Surfers. Blurring grade levels contributed to the change in nomenclature for the school and community. Built-in flexibility between the stages allowed students to be extended to higher stages than their chronological age would suggest. This was possible because of the broader inclusivity of the stages and the two-year cyclical curriculum-planning model that was established, ensuring that all students were exposed to core topics and competencies.

Planning is undertaken on a shared basis in stage teams. Teachers from each stage work in co-ordinated groups called 'stage meetings'. I have been particularly impressed with their quality and breadth of decision-making. Staff are quickly taking ownership for the staging process and exercise leadership that is having a positive impact on the school organization.

The change has been established in the formal policy arena. The school council approved a policy on staging at the end of 1999. This will ensure that later administrators will maintain the process until such time as an approved modification can be authenticated. Ownership for staging has been generally accepted by staff. However, further energy needs to be expended on developing community awareness.

The year 2000 witnessed a renewed emphasis on outcome-based learning by the department of education, with new programmes being developed according to this model. Since staging required an outcome-based approach, teachers have found the organization's expectations easier to accommodate.

THE PROBLEMS

Staff resistance

The main reasons for staff resistance were fear of the unknown, loss of control and the need for security. Many staff had been in the school for years and had experienced a number of administrative changes. Many were sceptical of new ideas, and multi-age was not popular with teachers because of their bias towards the familiar and the assumption that it required more time in planning and implementation. An emphasis on individual differences allowed me to establish multi-age. Staff who did not accept it after a concerted re-education process were given the opportunity to move to another more traditional school. This was expedited by staffing officers who took the view that teachers should not stay at a particular school for too long. Therefore, changes in staff enabled the move to staging to occur more successfully than if existing staff had remained in the school.

Community resistance

The community had an attachment to the traditional methods of teaching and learning and was suspicious of change. The change to multi-age was easier in Musgrave Hill because of the socio-economic influence and the unwillingness of the community generally to participate in school decision-making. The rate of change was slow and therefore it was more easily absorbed. Firstly, only a few classes were multi-age. Then the junior school, with the most proficient teachers taking this section, ensured the increasing popularity of multi-age. The next change came with the senior stage. Because most people acknowledged there was very little difference between Grades 6 and 7, little community resistance occurred. The final step was the biggest one, where I expected the greatest resistance. However, when the school moved to staging, it was generally accepted by the community, or more correctly, by those who took an interest in the school. This last step was accompanied by information sessions using external facilitators.

Curriculum co-ordination

Multi-age requires the curriculum to be co-ordinated differently from graded schools. If a cohesive curriculum structure is not imposed school-wide, each class will go in its own direction. This becomes difficult to reign in once it is established. Staging, on the other hand, being a whole-school approach, demands curriculum co-ordination. Leadership and curriculum management were the responsibility of the new deputy principal. The main reason for her appointment was to introduce a curriculum emphasis. Her personal commitment to multi-age and her expertise as an advisory teacher enabled me to have confidence in her curriculum work in a stage-based learning school.

LEADERSHIP STYLE AND APPROACH

For me, leadership is different from management, but good management encompasses leadership. Management is concerned with planning, organizing, leading, controlling, information gathering, decision-making and communicating. Leadership is an integral part of management, yet distinct. Leaders are not always good managers. In the case of change and innovation that the principal has initiated, leadership and management are intertwined and both are equally necessary to achieve success. Seven features of my management style are important.

Balance between structure and consideration

Ever since my early studies in behavioural theories of leadership, I have been excited about the idea of balancing initiating structure and consideration. The change to staging required support in the form of in-service training, precise communication, clear policies and guidelines. Without such a structure, the change would have been less directional and slower. Consideration was necessary to support all teachers in their coping strategies. Individual support was provided by encouragement and personal availability through peer support programmes, co-operative teaching and mentor schemes.

Because the change was occurring within a low socio-economic area, staff required high levels of consideration because there were other demanding issues such as behaviour management, lack of resources and an absence of parental support. By developing a depth of leadership through programme management, staff had opportunities to exercise their own leadership skills in a supportive environment. This strategy developed greater ownership of the changes as they were not originally initiated from the bottom up. In such circumstances, high consideration is necessary to ensure that staff morale is maintained, providing the resilience necessary to weather any storm.

Changing the structure and consideration mix provides me with the flexibility to respond to different situations in different ways. One situation may require a greater emphasis on procedures, information statements and evaluation, whilst another may require personal support and encouragement.

Vision

There is no leadership without vision. Vision to me is instilling and enthusing others to such a degree that they are persuaded and are willing to climb aboard. In the beginning there was no vision about staging. As the clarity of vision developed, so too did the number of people wishing to be part of the change. On reflection, it is difficult to be explicit about how the vision developed. In fact, staging was a collaborative vision that grew out of the circumstances of multi-age in Musgrave Hill, the education department's emphasis on staging, Mike Middleton's address and the arrival of a new deputy principal.

I spend considerable time talking to key individuals about the vision, where we are going and how this will impact on students. This provides opportunities to engage individuals in the visioning process. If an individual leader has all the vision, it will only last for as long as that person is leading. The aim of every leader should be to have a shared vision. Strategies I employ to promote a shared vision include:

- ensuring that the administration team is of one accord with the vision;
- using all available communication opportunities to promote the vision, such as newsletters, staff meetings, the media and individual discussions;
- encouraging all staff to be committed to the vision.

Empower

Empowering others enables the change process to have a wider ownership. Opportunities for individual staff to make decisions and to contribute to the direction of change will help ensure that it is long lasting. In the staging process, staff were empowered by being placed in curriculum teams to develop their teaching programmes for the following year. Releasing them from their classes enabled them to work uninterrupted on the task, strengthened their understanding of the change and created new networks for the following year.

The new procedure, introduced in 2000, allowed stage teams to participate in whole-school curriculum decision-making. This was a significant shift because it redirected energy away from the key learning areas, subjects, and focused it with renewed vigour on the integrated model. The curriculum leadership that developed within the staff enabled the school to embrace staging quickly and effectively.

Empowering occurs through the process of delegation and participative decision-making. Ultimately, successful change is dependent on those responsible for its implementation. They need to believe in it, have the skills to undertake it and be given the resources to make it happen.

Embrace change

My leadership shows a willingness to embrace change and encourage others to do likewise. Reflection on practice and questioning the present situation provides the springboard to change. Being receptive to change and willing to learn from it helps organizations to be successful. Embracing change releases creativity. When individuals or groups undertake transformation and move beyond their comfort zone, growth flourishes.

Of the three main change strategies, force (coercion), empirical (rational) and normative (re-educative), it is the last that I strive to reflect. The normative, re-educative strategy, although requiring considerable time investment, identifies and establishes values and assumptions from which support for change will naturally occur.

Staging required the school and community to understand the value of individual difference and that a focus of gradedness brings with it a number of negative outcomes. The re-education of the staff and community was necessary to achieve success. At Musgrave Hill the staff accepted the values and assumptions that underpinned staging. The community, on the other hand, was difficult to engage and was therefore not fully committed to the new direction that the school was taking. In time, and by continually emphasizing the difference of the Musgrave Hill state school educational programme, community understanding and acceptance will occur.

Individual integrity

It is essential for leaders to display integrity. I believe that leadership is not only about one's own integrity but also its promotion amongst staff. Maintaining appropriate ethical values by emphasizing the importance of the child through the promotion of individual difference builds integrity. By bringing individual difference into all that we do and evaluating our actions and planning by this measure, we build integrity into the organization.

Personal power

It is necessary to influence a school community to move it beyond a certain point. Influence is a form of power. My preferred mode is through the use of personal power, with its strands of expert and reference power. Expert power relates to the expert knowledge that I possess. My background in multi-age is extensive and is used to justify the change through rational debate. Reference power is the capability to influence people because of their desire to identify personally and positively with me. Such power is built by maintaining good interpersonal relations, supporting staff and community, displaying consistent integrity and seeking out the staff who will provide the best fit for the school and community. Personal power as a form of influence is longer lasting than the other forms of power. However, one downside is that using it takes longer to effect change, as was illustrated by the change to staging. This has taken six years.

Achievement oriented

The process is important, but if it does not have an outcome it can lack direction. In the early years of changing the school I did not have a focus on outcomes. I merely took every available opportunity to establish multi-age and positively promote non-gradedness. In those years the emphasis was, as it is now, on individual difference. This became the integrating device that enabled staging to become the legitimate end.

Now staging has been fully implemented at Musgrave Hill, it has become necessary to set achievement targets in the areas of planning, learning and community commitment. Continually striving to establish this change requires a vigilant awareness of influencing factors and levels of achievement in the identified areas.

IN CONCLUSION

My emphasis in leadership has been to transform the school organization into one that promotes the individual difference of the child, the teacher and the community member in the context of a multi-age school. To achieve this end I utilized a number of leadership strategies that attempted to cater for situational needs as they arose. The most significant factor that created successful change, apart from the leader, was the quality and commitment of teachers responsible for classroom implementation.

My leadership relies on collaboration and the synergy that flows from quality decision-making. Such a process gives opportunities for leadership to flourish in depth, thus ensuring sustained success.

5

Networking the independent brain

JILL CLOUGH

My teaching experience has all been in girls' schools, ranging from large city grammar schools to small, rural and boarding. My first significant learning came from
working alongside a head teacher who followed one of the country's first 20-day
management training courses. She carried out a school self-review which highlighted the complexity and ambiguity of a school's culture.

Rapid promotion, and head teachers who gave me excellent opportunities, led
to my first headship in 1987 in a small independent girls' boarding and day school.
I found the need to change the culture of both staff and pupils. The task was to
encourage staff to use their own independent professional judgement and to persuade the girls that they should set no ceiling to their aspirations. The drive for
improvement was almost wholly fuelled by the struggle to arrest declining numbers
in a boarding market.

I felt personally estranged by the fact that pupils came from very privileged homes
and tended to assume, not surprisingly, that they would inherit the earth. I wanted
them to understand that inheritance has to be worked for. Whilst I knew perfectly
well that they would probably lead cushioned lives, I believed in 'whole-brain education' and used Howard Gardner's concept of multiple intelligences as a guiding
principle for an integrated approach to managing education as a whole. In a boarding school, this had a particular resonance. Teachers had to be persuaded that their

influence extended over the whole of their pupils' lives, because the school was also a home. In fact we improved the school's public examination results by focusing on the value of extracurricular activities. This was my first chance to prove that real success comes from finding the right target.

WIMBLEDON HIGH SCHOOL

I started at Wimbledon High School (WHS) as head in 1995 and, in doing so, joined a corporate culture that has beliefs closer to my own. There was a passion for equality of opportunity for girls. My experiences in boarding education, nonetheless, profoundly affected my attitude to what can and should be accomplished in a day school. It gave me a clearer understanding of the many cultures, overlapping and conflicting, which each pupil experiences as a matter of course and must learn to handle. I had discovered that the leadership role is also inevitably a teaching role and is therefore transformational in nature.

THE SOCIO-ECONOMIC CONTEXT

Wimbledon High School belongs to the Girls' Day School Trust (GDST), 26 schools spread across the country with similar objectives. They provide single-sex education for intelligent girls in an academically selective environment, as far as possible regardless of their ability to pay. The normal ages of entry to the school are 4, 11 and 16 years.

Major financial matters are administered centrally by GDST. This keeps the fees relatively low and enables schools to offer bursaries to some pupils. The central control of salaries, fees, resources and building developments establishes common standards across the country. This means that individual schools cannot respond to their immediate market by decisions related to materials and facilities. Whilst the catchment area for WHS includes some deprived areas, there is also great affluence. For historic reasons the school has few bursaries. Nonetheless, in joining the GDST, all parents accept the implicit social agenda that the schools will be economically run so that children from other backgrounds will not be denied access.

The immediate local educational context is highly competitive. We are surrounded by oversubscribed selective maintained girls' schools, single-sex and mixed comprehensives with excellent reputations and many independent schools both single-sex and co-educational. Immediate competitors include the most prestigious schools in the country. They charge much higher fees than the GDST and are thus able to provide more resources. On the other hand, a substantial number of families deliberately choose WHS for its relatively wide social range. There is a strong sense of the need for social justice within the parent body, although this is not reflected in a commitment to comprehensive education.

Within the school's locality there is plenty of ethnic diversity, with recent immigrants and families whose cultural backgrounds reflect the intermarriages of generations. This diversity is fully reflected in the school and is important to everyone associated with it. There is no display of personal wealth. The girls set a high priority on social and community service. They believe it to be one of the school's most important qualities. It was one of the major factors attracting me to the school, making it easy, for instance, to introduce World Challenge international expeditions to the pupils and parents, who understood and endorsed its principles.

The head controls the salary budget, a day-to-day maintenance budget, and is free to determine the curriculum. GDST expects that the schools will in general follow the National Curriculum. The GDST also has its own educational adviser to work with the head teachers in its schools. Strategic development planning is essential. It is by this means that the GDST can be persuaded to allocate capital funds to the school, usually on the basis of plans for curriculum development.

I recruit all the teachers, who must be fully qualified professionally, apart from the deputy head and the head of the junior school. The relationship between head and governors is inevitably distant. The council of the GDST is the executive group governing all 26 schools and its decisions apply to all. Each school has a body of local governors who provide advice, which at WHS is of outstanding quality, but which has no executive authority. I can and do ask for advice and assistance from my local governors, but am not bound to do so.

THE SCHOOL IN 1995

Factors affecting the school in 1995 included:

* relatively high examination results;

- a very short tenure by my predecessor, less than three years, because she had lost her sight almost as soon as joining the school;
- her handover commentary that there were a number of issues that she had not tackled because of her personal problems;
- her predecessor having enlarged the senior school considerably in the previous 10 years, with some new building to house the greater numbers, but a desperate need for more facilities, to meet the burgeoning needs of the curriculum;
- a three-year strategic development plan which was coming to an end, and had identified the urgent need for a new junior school building, preferably on a separate site.

This last aspect would have provided the younger children with more suitable premises, including specialist rooms, and allowed the older students to expand into the vacated space. Concealed among these problems were more complex issues.

MANAGEMENT

The most challenging matter was managerial. The senior management team (SMT) itself had weathered a great deal of unintended and unstructured change and was adept at crisis management, day-to-day organization of the school and emotional support for the staff. There was, however, no clear means of relating the decisions of the SMT to the work of the staff as a whole. SMT meetings were very co-operative in tone and procedures were clear, but previous head teachers had kept a great deal within their own authority, thus limiting real decision-making by the group. Many of my most urgent questions went unanswered. For instance, who was responsible for monitoring and advising on the development of individual pupils, how were teaching standards raised and who was involved in making major decisions? In effect, I found not a team, but a collaborative group.

As is very common in schools of this type, there were many heads of department. A flat structure existed in which there was mutual respect, but ideas and judgements were not shared, tested and used to inform a decision-making process to support the school's development as a whole. The corollaries were a highly developed sense of personal responsibility in all members of staff, whatever their status, and yet a crucial deficit in the tracking, monitoring and managing of the individual development of pupils. Staff worked hard to enable their pupils to achieve high standards, but there was no system to facilitate collaboration between teachers to raise standards.

CURRICULUM REVIEW

Individual departments made decisions about their curriculum areas without discussing with others the impact on pupils, or on the school as a whole. This pointed to the same lack of a shared vision of how education should be managed and led. One of the recent appointments to the SMT was the curriculum co-ordinator, but it was hard for her to develop the role in the absence of a suitable system.

RELATIONSHIP WITH THE JUNIOR SCHOOL

The head of the junior school was not really involved in the life of the SMT at all, although she was responsible for recruiting both pupils and staff in the junior school. She attended some, but not all, meetings of the SMT, yet the junior school supplied almost half of the intake for the senior school. In effect, the educational standards and assumptions of a substantial cohort of the school had been formed in their earlier years in the school, but this influenced few policies.

There was an excellent informal network of communication about pastoral matters with all staff committed to the social and emotional welfare of the pupils and readily sharing information. There was no means, however, of integrating this with managing the same pupils' academic development. Despite excellent public examination results, too many girls were tending to underachieve relative to their ability. I knew from my boarding school days how inextricably bound emotional well-being is to academic success, what we now regard as the emotional quotient (EQ).

I could find no means within the school, academically successful though it was, of keeping my finger on the pulse of the core activity of teaching and learning. Nor could I see how to engage in detailed debate about overall educational aims and developments with the leaders of learning amongst the staff. There was no formal reflective mode within the school.

THE PRESSURES

There was a very competitive and watchful local community. The physical environment of the school had a planning blight, bred by years of uncertainty. The staff had learned to live with uncertainty of all kinds by doing their work independently, which was good, and hoping that no more uncertainties would be introduced, which was fantasy. The school was oversubscribed and had too many teachers. The problems associated with recruitment and retention at both levels had never been taken seriously.

In 1995, therefore, the major tasks were to:

- find systems that would allow staff to work more effectively and collaboratively, so that we could generate a holistic approach to the pupils;
- find a way in which teaching and learning could sit at the heart of the process, with improved professional development and renewed understanding of personal teaching and learning styles;
- make the best possible use of the school's 4–18 cohort, which would mean changing the culture of the SMT itself;
- establish the significance of the role of the head of the junior school;
- ensure that parents would understand and subscribe to any changes in the school.

SIGNIFICANT CHANGES

After five years, the following has been achieved:

- the junior school has been rebuilt on the same site;
- substantial redevelopment is now taking place within the structure of the senior school, including some facilities formerly used by the juniors;
- redefinition of SMT roles;
- a faculty structure in the senior school, led by the deputy head who is in charge of teaching and learning;
- an equivalent structure evolving in the juniors;
- a forum for curriculum review;
- a school assessment officer, who leads on monitoring pupil development through the use of a databank of objective evidence as well as personal experience and judgement, and who also manages the special educational needs policy, from the gifted to the dyspraxic to the disturbed;
- significant impact of ICT (information and communications technology) on the life and systems in the school;
- commitment to achieving accreditation as Investors in People;
- varieties of thinking skills taught throughout the school, as one of the key ways of improving teaching and skills;
- a new role for the head of the junior school, leading the SMT on 'the school of the future'.

The last aspect has resulted in her acceptance as a key member of the SMT. Her ideas, and through her the insights of her team of junior school staff, now affect the overall policy-making of the school.

Still under review are:

- the senior school tutorial system, which needs to bring together academic and pastoral monitoring, focus on emotional security and stability, and to engender independent, resilient learning and resourcefulness;
- subject specialization for junior school teachers with a focus for 11-year-olds on fewer teachers managing the cohort in order to tackle regression on transfer;
- the understanding of subject specialists in order to assess the significance of the information revolution for their own status as teachers;
- a flexible approach to the curriculum, not only the new Advanced level system, but the management of accelerated learning, critical thinking, distance learning, integration of the informal curriculum and whatever else the ICT revolution may liberate in learning strategies;
- roles of the SMT, as we are still not fully a team.

In short, managing uncertainty is now more important than ever.

MAIN PROBLEMS

Changing roles

These still engender anxiety and uncertainty. I have been slow to realize that the ability to slip flexibly between roles is not instinctively shared by all teachers, and that clever, well-educated people still cannot easily re-conceive their roles. Nowhere has this challenge been more crucial than within the management team itself. Asking colleagues to accept the implications of being a 4–18 school triggered off unexpected emotional responses, most of which were directly related to sensitivity about roles and expectations.

Transforming teachers into tutors

This remains an uphill struggle. What teachers personally experience about their pupils has to be related to objective assessment data as well as the knowledge of pupils' learning styles and needs. Teachers must learn to modify their teaching in the light of this understanding as well as helping pupils to set appropriate targets. The complexity of the role is embraced by many, resisted by some.

Rebuilding the junior school

Sharing the site has imposed considerable physical and emotional stress on the entire school community. In fact, the physical conditions have far-reaching consequences. Providing a set of pigeon-holes for pupils has transferred responsibility from staff to pupils and released the staff from the chore of being messengers. Losing a staff dining room has threatened the egalitarian quality of the staff culture so seriously that I set a high priority on recovering the facility. In terms of Maslow's hierarchy of human needs, the community needs self-actualization as much as the individuals.

Consultation

Staff easily forget that they have been consulted even if everyone has not been present simultaneously for the debate. It is fatally easy for the head to manipulate decisions by appearing to be the democratic leader of a meeting of a large number of staff. Debate in small groups and delegated decision-making, allied to delegated responsibility, is both rewarding and successful, because the proposals are of a higher order than those that emerge from a plenary session. But the culture of many schools is still to expect that all teachers, but not the rest of the staff, will attend a staff meeting and reach a consensus. However consultative any alternative process may be, the head is likely to be deemed despotic if not publicly seen to be listening. This also depends on the other messengers who relay information on behalf of the head. Shared culture and beliefs are important ingredients of success.

Managing change

This is an art form. There are few circumstances in which staff believe that they have been involved in determining a change, probably because no one wants to expend energy on the change when the moment comes. Too many crises are automatically dealt with on a daily basis for anyone to have hoarded the additional energy necessary to implement the change. Perhaps change is an emotional rather than an intellectual experience, hence the analogy with art.

SUCCESSES

New roles

Many staff are exhilarated by their new roles and they challenge me. Rarely is a request on my part simply carried out because I am the head teacher. Their questions come from a real desire to understand the issue under debate and, by constructive criticism, to generate a better idea. Teachers are very honest with me. I want challenging staff because I want effective role models for pupils. This makes it harder to lead the staff, but more rewarding.

Teaching standards

These have risen markedly. When new teachers are recruited from other schools, we usually find that WHS staff are the better teachers. The task is to replace them with those who are as good. The staff know this and are immensely proud of it.

Standards of learning

We are generating a more independent and challenging cohort of students and believe that this arises from a persistent, patient focus on these standards. Recently I asked a 10-year-old pupil how the school had given her confidence. 'People keep asking me for my opinion,' was the reply.

Pupil support policy

The policy is grasped and understood by most of the staff, who accept the need to look at the whole nature of the student. Recently our General Certificate of Secondary Education (GCSE) students have exceeded all expectations and teachers recognize that this derives from a detailed, patient approach, on an individual basis, in which staff help students to reflect on their strengths and goals, making discreet use of all the available information.

PERSONAL LEADERSHIP STYLE AND APPROACH

Details count. Though I was a very impatient child, I now set high value on what might appear small scale. I believe that any school structure must accommodate the fact no one is more important than the most part-time member of staff because, for the pupils with that teacher, what occurs in the classroom is of lasting significance. I probably feel this the more because so many part-time women teachers contribute hugely to the lives of their schools as they juggle family commitments with children or elderly relatives.

I have always wanted to be in touch with the core life of the school by teaching, a highly effective way of sampling the process. Keats wrote that poetry must be 'felt on one's pulses' and I need to 'feel' the school around me, its daily language, interrelationships, attitudes to authority, to learning and to independence. The list of what can be discovered by teaching is long.

I have needed to find ways of maintaining conversations without undermining delegated authority, realizing slowly that when someone talks to the head teacher she feels that whatever has been discussed is in some way mandated. I could make life easier by engaging in fewer discussions, but I know that I am setting the tone for the conversation of the school, developing an excited and enthusiastic experience of learning in which we all collaborate.

The head has to be a role model for teachers and pupils alike, especially in managing her own authority and endorsing the talents of others. The leadership role is at the heart of this, since everyone possesses leadership attributes and all need to feel the weight of being taken seriously.

At the start of my first headship, I read Tom Peters' *In Search of Excellence*, a study of the characteristics of the world's leading companies. His conclusions influenced me profoundly, especially the need for 'simultaneous loose–tight properties'. One should give autonomy, but have a tight, central core of belief. Everyone is entitled to small-scale experiments and to support from a champion if these fail. There is a fundamental elasticity about an organization working in this way, which initially seems to make teachers nervous, but which is also liberating. Another of the Peters' precepts is 'Ready. Fire. Aim'. This breeds even more nervousness but, if one is confident about what should happen and eager to push ahead, the moment may be lost if one pauses. I am driven by the awareness that for pupils the irreplaceable time is now.

Tom Peters comments that one must socialize incoming managers. They will have been appointed as leaders of a strong culture which may, if we are not sensitive and adept, repress the very qualities for enlarging and strengthening that culture, for which they have been appointed. Thus, inconsequential meetings can be engineered to ensure that new teachers feel included immediately.

My first reaction if an event has not gone well, or if staff are agitated, is to look at the system within which we are requiring them to operate. Hard-working people often automatically cling to or attribute blame. Usually, the dislocation is not directly under the head's control and the frustration of having to let other people sort it out can be acute. I understand more than ever that in the simultaneously over- and underplanned educational world that we inhabit, you cannot solve other people's problems unless you become the other people. You have to find ways of helping them to solve the problems for themselves.

My latest understanding of this axiom derives from learning to teach a philosophy programme to 10-year-olds. The programme focuses on allowing pupils to discover the right questions to ask. I had to learn a new methodology, which filled me with the uncertainty I perceive in other staff. What I learn justifies the time spent teaching, since it helps me to understand the leadership role more clearly, as well as providing pedagogical insights.

Although I often seem preoccupied by systems, my energy is increasingly spent on helping individuals to use their authority. I have to remember not to make an inspired decision that cuts across that authority. I am used to apologizing. Clear job descriptions are essential, but these alone do not confer authority. The authority comes from understanding the culture and one's places in it. I use the plural deliberately because most staff have many roles. Laboratory technicians teach, the school administrator is an adept counsellor, the caterer goes on stage with the head of science in a karaoke competition. This versatility is their delight and brings the school's behaviour code to life for the pupils. Staff and pupils alike feel the liberating effects of knowing that they are valued from many aspects, together with the insecurity of having to deal with shifting boundaries all the time. The more I understand this, the more I talk about it, to make the boundary changes less threatening, more familiar and more homely.

Since I have learned to teach thinking skills, I want all staff to have the same experience, not just for the impact on student learning, but for the potential transformation in their teaching. Having grasped a congenial methodology they will want to remodel their teaching. We seem to be using several different thinking skills programmes so there should be plenty of choice. I do not know where this will lead except to even more challenging pupils and staff. I know that I am the driving force behind such plans but there are enough like minds on the staff to take them forward and I can trust others to conduct radical investigations and produce unexpected proposals.

I am still looking for the appropriate mental model for systems that allow the organic life of the school to develop sturdily. One with which I feel comfortable was produced by Louise Stoll. It looks rather like an amoeba. Within the outer amorphous boundary of the school are all the individual spheres of experience, like atoms swimming in a medium.

Another management model that appeals to me is Charles Handy's suggestion of a constellation of stars. This describes the collective but independent work of barristers in chambers or doctors in practice, and certainly gives gravitas to the professionalism of teachers, many of whom are still Brodie-like to their pupils. I treat them as stars. They need to be.

Teachers collaborate in ways unfamiliar to Miss Brodie. The stars of the teaching profession have to be continually forming themselves into different task forces. Each pupil in the secondary phase has her special constellation of stars. Every member of one pupil's star cluster has to be equally at home in someone else's constellation. There may be at least 15 graduates interacting with each student at any one time, apart from other specialists who might also have advice to offer. Handy's model for this is a network. In practice, it is difficult to achieve because each teacher is handling too many experiences simultaneously to be able to network on the scale that the task requires.

There is a looseness about the model which ignores the tight structure of the school's values, to which everyone needs to refer with absolute confidence. The comment, 'We do things like this, don't we?' has to receive a chorus of assent. Handy points out that the network approach is very expensive and my school, like most, burns blood and muscle, not fat.

A creative, mental model is that of the brain itself. Having recently heard Professor Susan Greenfield describing the growth of neural networks as unique and transforming for each individual, and having read Danah Zohar's *Rewiring the Corporate Brain*, I have concluded that this is the best working model for the life of a school. The networks are forged between individual members of staff, pupils, parents and governors, through all the permutations one can imagine. The brain's chemistry ensures that any determined network will create a chemical change, which transforms the nature of the individual. Thus, we become unique.

I have yet to work out how to translate this model into some practical management system, except that it involves trusting other people's decisions and assuming the best rather than the worst about their behaviour. I find this as hard as everyone else does, since I lose my sense of control if I delegate as completely as my principles imply. But in terms of brain function, some of my best thinking is subconscious, non-verbal and unexpected. Once a new neural network has become chemically viable, the brain quietens. Another attractive analogy is that more parts of the brain are involved in any one operation than is at first apparent.

So, in a school, activity in one area has repercussions that may transform the whole. Staff who stay late after school performances to help pupils pick up litter and stack chairs have as much to do with the sense of worth these pupils imbibe as anything printed in a mission statement. I make daily decisions on this basis and sweep the floor when required. I can see that many of my overt actions are symbolic.

Emotional stability is essential if people are to be confident learners when things are changing so fast. The climate has to be forgiving. I want to achieve a sense of collective purpose based on a common vision of human potential. Intelligence is not fixed. Faith moves mountains. Whole-brain development can produce startling academic outcomes. I know that staff are beginning to believe this because we have had bad times when the only sane focus has been looking after their emotional well-being to the best of our ability. The students on whom we have lavished this attention have grown into people whom it is a joy to educate. Their public examination results have been wonderful too, certainly no coincidence.

I have not succeeded in persuading the staff to use consistently a system for recording any kind of student excellence: effort, achievement and personal goal-setting. However, they consistently and abundantly give of their time. The information revolution makes me work faster and attempt more. It has the same effect on everyone else. Time gets eaten up if I am not careful, or I am not careful enough. I feel more than ever the importance of setting everything else aside in order to concentrate on the person who is with me.

The implications for leadership are profound. Zohar points out that the quantum principle that replaces Newtonian science is complex, chaotic and uncertain. Just when you feel you have set up a clear system, which everyone understands and can operate, something changes and uncertainty returns. This is the fundamental principle of the new learning, I suppose. However, instead of fretting about it, I accept what the parents say when they bring their children to school: 'I want her to be happy.' Children have no problems in coping with change if we give them our considered attention. The key is to look for what is unambiguous in an ever-changing environment. Praise, attention to the individual, taking time, being able to take a strong moral stand, being seen to struggle over finding the balance between the needs of the individual and the needs of the whole, believing in yourself and in others, all of these are important. I always picture the best.

It seems an odd management principle after all these years, but I now live with the personal discipline of trying to keep my word, making sure that I pay equal attention to everyone regardless of age or status, and trusting other people's judgement as much as my own. At least, with regard to the last, I can be confident that I will give them as hard a time as I give myself.

6

'Thorough winning clarity'

Mike Hardacre

I started teaching in the late 1960s at a school in south-east England that served overspill estates from the East End of London. Most of the families had been re-housed to the estates. Academic and pastoral leadership posts followed in Lancashire. Both these schools served multi-ethnic areas that were also experiencing above average levels of social deprivation. From there I moved to the West Midlands as a deputy head teacher in an area that suffered from 40 per cent unemployment, in the wake of the closure of the steel industry in the 1980s.

Finally, in 1988 I became head teacher of Coppice High School, an 11–18 comprehensive school serving a 1960s' council estate suffering from the effects of long-term unemployment. I was appointed when the Secretary of State for Education had settled the education service's long-running dispute with the professional associations by sweeping away the Burnham Committee, which negotiated teachers' salaries and conditions of service, and imposing the 1265-hour contract on teachers. At the same time the service saw the introduction of the National Curriculum and Local Management of Schools (LMS). During this period, we also witnessed the slow death of the government-sponsored Technical and Vocational Education Initiative (TVEI) and a sharp increase in central government control over the content, process and financing of education.

This combination of events changed the face of school, local education authority (LEA) and government management of the education service. Gone, along with changes in the composition of governing bodies, was the ability of LEAs to control appointments, minor building works, promotions, in-school budget distribution, professional development and the curriculum. These were now in the hands of the head teacher and governing body.

COPPICE HIGH SCHOOL

THE SCHOOL CONTEXT

I inherited a school in decline. There were 170 pupils leaving and 99 arriving, few of whom had made the school a first choice. There was no management structure. Some staff members, who held seemingly commensurate responsibilities, were paid different salaries. The school had a senior management team (SMT) of three deputy heads and two senior teachers, which had been appropriate when it had 1100 pupils. They knew that change had to occur. Staff and governors wanted change, but they did not want anyone to be upset.

The local community had lost faith in the ability of the school to deal with macho 16-year-old boys, whom they perceived as characterizing the pupil ethos. The school, in line with local policy on special needs provision, had a special resource area containing 25 pupils who had been statemented for mild learning difficulties. There were enough spare places at the nearest two LEA schools to absorb the 600 Coppice pupils. During my first years of headship, the LEA produced a rationalization plan with several options, all but one of which identified the school for closure.

THE PATH FORWARD

Two gurus have shaped my thinking about managing systems and institutions. Both were admired rather than liked. The clarity of purpose and logical thinking of each enabled them to deal dispassionately with issues. The first, the Earl of Strafford, instituted the policy of 'thorough' in the administration of Charles I. The policy can be defined as a rigorous and unitary administration, which acted impartially in everyone's interests.

I resolved, in the spirit of 'thorough', that the school needed a clear purpose, that its management and administrative structures should serve that purpose and be made to work efficiently and caringly in the interests of all. If necessary, this meant dealing effectively with sectional interests that existed in the staffroom, pupil body and the community served by the school.

The second guru conditioned how I moved towards that aim. Field Marshal Montgomery wrote in the opening chapter of his memoirs, 'People may not agree with what I say, but at least they know what I am saying. '

I was not resolving a 17th-century king's problems with a burgeoning bourgeoisie, nor was I leading a ferocious military campaign. However, the main principles of clarity of purpose, efficiency of administration, equity and honesty in dealing with others were ones that would change radically the face of the school.

THE TASKS

The school held briefings every morning, for all staff who were not on duty. As a response to the imposition of the 1265-hours contract, teachers had been expected to sign in to register their presence. At my first briefing I told the staff two things. One was a simple statement of philosophy, and the other a pragmatic gesture. The latter was to abolish the 'signing-in' book. I believed that the book subliminally de-professionalized the staff and treated them as if they were working on an assembly line. The gesture was greeted with approval.

The philosophical statement was to remind colleagues that Coppice was a school, not a social work agency. Our purpose was to produce educational success and we should deal with behavioural and social problems only in order to equip pupils for learning. This was important, in that it made clear to staff that the core activity was teaching. The school may have to deal with the behavioural and academic consequences of social dislocation, but it cannot deal with the causes. My first purpose was to establish this simple message for all staff, pupils and governors. No school can solve the ills of the world. The purpose of a school is to build a learning community. It enabled me to move the agenda away from what I perceived to be a community that cared, and cared deeply, to one in which a learning ethos became pre-eminent. The school continued to take great care of its pupils, but for a purpose, providing them with conditions in which to learn. Having established this simple precept for staff and pupils, over a period of time, I set standards of lesson quality for staff. If they were teaching at a standard less than they would want for their own children, it was not good enough.

The school needed to change its emphasis. The history of low and intermediate levels of disruptive behaviour and petty vandalism needed tackling more overtly. This led to a degree of confrontation that could not be shirked. A number of pupils came from difficult backgrounds where parents had only marginal control over the behaviour of their offspring. A significant number were already subject to social service and police intervention. The school's catchment area was one where inter- and intra-family disputes were rarely settled by rational discussion. The results were brought into school. There was little option but to deal with the consequences. The message for pupils and parents alike was that their own difficulties must not erupt at school. I took a firm line over behaviour. All available sanctions were used, although at that time exclusion was administratively easier. These events applied to a small but significant minority of pupils, but unless firmly but equitably handled, they can come to characterize the school in the minds of the local community. Experience tells me, however, that exclusion rarely solves the individual pupil's problem but is often used *pour encourager les autres*.

When we involve parents in the disciplinary process we cannot dictate what may happen when the information goes home. Punishment has to be tempered with justice for the offender as well as those offended against. This is sometimes a very difficult lesson for some members of our community.

CHANGING THE STRUCTURES

I then turned to the structural issues. The purpose of changing the management structure was to provide a flow of information upwards so that policy decisions could be made on an informed basis. Corporate decisions, made after a full exchange of views, were then given to the curriculum area managers who were asked to introduce the new policy. I have never believed in lengthy job descriptions with a multitude of clauses. They should be short and clear. People work best within an overall framework that maximises their ability to behave professionally in matters of curriculum choice and delivery. I did not know all the details of curriculum content; that was the task of the curriculum area managers. However, I did know something of curriculum delivery but persuading staff to alter their teaching style was a long-term issue.

The new management structure was based on the simple premise that nobody should hold more than one responsibility and that there should be parity of salary, as far as was possible, between similar posts. The academic structure was complemented by a pastoral organization based on similar precepts. The meeting pattern was changed. The curriculum managers and SMT met four times a term as, initially, the academic board. There was cross-representation by one person from a similarly constituted pastoral board which met twice a term. This helped to ensure a continuous flow of information upwards, downwards and laterally. It helped the school to maintain a unity of purpose and provided good opportunities for discussion

As a management team, we would bring papers to the academic board where they could be talked through. Where agreement was reached, a revised paper would be published for all staff, which curriculum managers would take through their area meetings. If agreement were not reached in the academic board, the SMT would ask for written comments and return with a modified paper. The decision would be made at the next academic board. Thus, papers would not be repeatedly modified at each meeting, never achieving the status of school policy. Policy was created quickly and widespread discussion was invited on its operation. This was then disseminated to the whole staff. The purpose was to set the climate for coherent change in which staff had a measure of control over delivery, as well as contributing to the creation of policy.

Staff meetings set the agenda for each half term, so that all the staff became familiar with the next set of issues, but whole staff meetings did not make decisions. This process meant that the SMT drove the agenda for the school. The purpose of the restructuring of management and meetings was to encourage the staff to subscribe fully to the school's main priorities. It was clear that, while this would produce the changes I believed necessary in the short term, the structure would subsequently need to be more flexible. The command economy model only works well for a short time but, given the school's starting point, it was accepted by the staff.

I used a series of standard letters on issues such as absence, lateness and underachievement that tutorial and subject staff could access. The letters were written in plain English and required only the insertion of the names of the student and teacher before being mailed. They ended with an invitation to contact the sender. The letters saved the office and the staff a great deal of time as well as making clear to parents that the school was determined to create a caring, educational community of which they were a part. In hindsight, I should have produced more letters about positive aspects of behaviour and achievement. They came later and had an even greater effect in changing student behaviour than the negative letters. While this may seem an obvious piece of psychology, it is something that schools are not always good at. Positive reinforcement is a more successful modifier of behaviour than criticism.

It was clear to me that the school needed a higher profile in its immediate community and in the local media. Many things happened that were extremely positive such as pupils winning competitions, gaining external certificates and participating in charity work. I resolved to write two press releases a week based on the positive achievements of pupils and staff. Though the potential range of stories is massive, it is difficult to predict what will capture the interest of the media. While this was a scattergun approach, it was successful in gaining media coverage. The school always ensured that press releases had eye-catching headlines and included quotes from a pupil, a member of staff and the head teacher. They contained a contact telephone number and an open invitation to come to school, take photographs and elicit further information. With digital cameras and online information transmission, I have no doubt that this process could now be greatly enhanced. The appearance of the school and its pupils in the media for positive reasons produces a tremendous synergy between parents, school and the community that raises everyone's self-esteem.

WORKING WITH PARTNERS

No head teacher can successfully manage change without the backing of the school's partners, but I believe that this cohesion should not be at the expense of a sound educational philosophy. While the pupils, parents, staff and community are important partners for the head teacher, the vital relationship, which ensures the future of the school, is the one between the head teacher and the governing body. The quality of the relationships between the head teacher and others will condition governors' perceptions of how the school is moving in relation to the philosophy they and the head teacher espouse.

Over my period of headship, the powers of governing bodies have been extended, largely at the expense of LEAs. I always tried to draw a clear line for governors between their philosophical and strategic responsibilities and the day-to-day management by the head teacher and staff. This is not always an easy task. Different schools will create structures with their governors that facilitate the creation and execution of policy. It was our view that 'a governor was a governor was a governor'. Apart from the statutory committees, there were no other committees of the governing body. Governors were fully involved in all policy decisions in meetings of the full governing body.

The first and appeal committees were a statutory necessity to deal with pupil and staff appeals against the decisions of the head teacher. They also discussed matters relating to redundancy, redeployment and premature retirement. Clearly these were matters where confidentiality and fair play were needed and could not be carried out in the open governors' meetings. I do not believe this approach to be unique, but it does place upon the head teacher the responsibility of being well prepared, writing simply and lucidly. It also implies explicitly that the governors' meeting is a forum for discussion before decisions are taken. The process can be exhausting and exhaustive. Head teachers need to trail issues and to work hard to ensure that governors do not drown in a sea of paper, consequently becoming less supportive. Many other schools have adopted a structure of committees, with the governing body being little more than a rubber-stamp. These are often successful and improving schools. The issue, however, is not the structure, but the development of a clear and lucid articulation of the school's vision. Clarity of written and oral communication, coupled with enthusiasm and hard work, can change the cultural perceptions of a school and its community.

MAINTAINING THE CHANGE DYNAMIC

If a dynamic for change is to be created and maintained, there needs to be a measure of control by the head teacher and SMT. In structural, academic, political and community terms the *status quo* is not an option. It is a truism that change does not occur unless everyone is aware that change has taken place. The head teacher's role in this is to initiate change, maintain the momentum and ensure that everyone knows that the changes are occurring. There is in this apparently simple process a range of affective domain work to be done by the head teacher and SMT. Some of that is reassurance about process and quality.

Pupils produce their best work in a climate of support and praise. This does not mean that criticism should not take place, but that it should occur in a nondestructive context. The creation of such a climate is the responsibility of the head teacher and the staff. Education exists to change student behaviour. What has to be created is an ethos of support for young people, while making clear the expectations of behaviour, work rate and attitude.

If all of this is true for pupils, it is even more important for staff. No head teacher should underestimate the power of positive reinforcement that individual words of praise can give. Time spent with an individual in one's office, informally offering praise and encouragement, brings untold benefits. Even when problems are occurring, it is better to start and end a conversation with what is going well and deal with issues for modification in between.

The task of management and leadership is to set the philosophy and ethos of the school and then to create the structures to put that into practice. Staff, both non-teaching and teaching, need to understand the basis on which the school is operating. It is the job of the SMT to encourage, cajole and ensure that staff are working in a way that is consistent with the value systems espoused by the leadership team.

PHILOSOPHY TO PRACTICALITY

The purpose of the routines and procedures of the school is to put the philosophy into practice so that the basic levels of behaviour establish a starting point for the education of pupils. It may seem obvious, but teaching pupils is a different process from educating them. Teaching is concerned with the transmission of knowledge. It is the school's base camp from which we move towards the summit of education. Teaching is a closed activity that involves, for the taught, a low risk. Educating is a high-risk activity. The process gives pupils options and allows them to make choices in the full knowledge of the consequences. Not all pupils or staff will respond to these opportunities and it is the task of the school leader to ensure that there is a safety net for the individual. This is a model of personal growth in an institutional setting that I regard as the highest aspiration. If it is done properly, good academic results will follow. Done poorly, and without conviction by all partners, it will fail.

In order to put these ambitions into practice, the importance of teamwork cannot be underestimated. The head teacher is responsible for many teams: pupils, teachers, non-teaching staff, governors, parents and the community. These teams have subdivisions. Their needs and aspirations, as well as those of the individuals in them, have to be balanced. In this, the role of the head teacher is like that of a conductor leading an orchestra. Each group contains individuals who exert influence and are, as the symbolic interactionists write, 'significant others'. Unless a head teacher is able to identify the significant others in each team, and either use them or nullify their influence, all will be lost.

The head teacher's most immediate grouping is the SMT and it is vitally important that this team has absolute unanimity of purpose, action and thought. Decisions, once made, must be adhered to. Private disagreement is inevitable, indeed essential, but the concept of collective responsibility must be pre-eminent. The *modus operandi* with other groups requires openness and a full exchange of information, commensurate with matters of confidentiality, in order to be successful. It is not always comfortable. Profound disagreement must be possible whilst still working together. The avoidance of disagreement as a purpose in itself is not healthy and is likely to produce compromise. The opposite proposition is also true. Conflict as a change mechanism has a short and unsuccessful history. The head teacher must try to ensure that there are simple goals to which all can subscribe and feel valued within the institution.

I am a great believer in simplicity and, without wishing to reduce the significance, there is no better or simpler method than to spend much of one's day walking the school! This simple technique of management by doing, as I prefer to think of it, is tremendously effective in giving the head teacher the opportunity to lead, coach and exert a degree of quality control over classroom and corridor interactions. No learning community can exist unless there is order in classrooms, on the corridors, in the grounds and, where applicable, in the community.

The creation of a learning community requires the school to create a climate of control over as much of its environment as possible. In the initial phase of headship I took it upon myself to see most parents who had a complaint. Some of these interviews were extremely difficult. Parents are on edge and need to be put at their ease. The head teacher needs to work through the anger and keep returning to the core issue of the pupil's behaviour in relation to the particular incident. Parents do not always understand that their child's behaviour can be anti-social and inappropriate and that there is no excuse for behaviour that disrupts the learning environment.

This extends to dealing, clearly and firmly, with the depredations of early evening motorcyclists, gangs of unemployed youths, young people excluded from other schools and those who like to climb up buildings. There are many such people in an urban environment that is suffering from structural decay. I did not hesitate to involve the local authority's legal department in order to ban the anti-social element from the school premises. This made life easier for the police to handle if further incursions took place.

The presence of the 'community bobby' on the governing body was extremely useful in terms of information exchange. This helped a large number of young people in the school's catchment to avoid becoming deeply embroiled in criminal activity. Police days were held, when the police came in *en masse* to talk to young people in personal and social education lessons, and to show off their motor cycles, horses and other equipment. These helped to change the pupils' and the community's perception of what the police could and could not do. After 12 years it can be said with confidence that the police enjoy a more positive relationship with the school's parents and their children than they had at the beginning. I have no doubt that skilled and sensitive work by the 'beat bobby', combined with a close relationship with the school, had a major impact. The area turned from one that was difficult to police, to one where criminal activity declined steadily.

There are several ways of knowing what is happening in a school. One is the data-rich methodology that can easily lead to a blame culture. This tends to produce a 'looking over the shoulder' culture that does not encourage risk-taking and is, I believe, damaging to education. It produces short-termism and quick fixes. It has its place in the system, but no head teacher should rely entirely upon data to monitor the progress of the school. Managing by doing means that the head teacher and SMT members must spend much of the school day out of their offices. This requires good administrative support. It also implies that most of the writing and interpretation of events by school leaders takes place outside the school day. Great commitment by the senior team is required and it is the head teacher's responsibility to create that commitment.

STRIKING AND KEEPING A BALANCE

School leaders need to be excellent time managers and a head teacher must establish a system that allows managers to manage. No secondary school can be run on the basis of a head teacher and classroom teachers without an intermediate management structure. There is a clear conflict of interest here. Normally the SMT, curriculum area managers and pastoral leaders are in those positions because they have proved themselves in the classroom. The head teacher must strike a balance for the senior staff between a teaching commitment and the managerial function. The head must be able to demonstrate expertise in interactions with the pupils, staff and others, treating people as the head would wish to be treated. Pupils particularly have a strong sense of justice and they, like staff, wish to be treated equitably. They need to be given support and praise. If the head teacher and senior team maintain this climate, pupils and staff will be better prepared to improve in situations when they get it wrong. It is a potential disaster if pupils and staff fail to understand when their actions are not consistent with the school's ethos. They should be left with a clear picture of what they did wrong, why it was wrong, what they can do to ensure there is no repetition, and without resentment about the correction. Life cannot be lived in some mythical zone of comfort.

As head teacher, one is the ultimate arbiter of student and professional standards. That can lead to some uncomfortable moments in dealing with staff, pupils, governors and parents. The head teacher cannot flinch from those moments, but must be seen to be fair. Fortunately, agreed procedures exist for the protection of the head as much as for everyone else.

A head teacher should be very clear both about his responsibilities and those of other members of staff. While it is the head teacher's task to be around the school, checking that its routines and procedures are operating, it is the responsibility of senior and middle managers to monitor the work of staff. If a head teacher finds, for example, that there is no evidence of homework being set by a teacher, there is a temptation to deal with it oneself at the earliest opportunity. It may be satisfying to believe that the head is the only person who can deal with the issue! However, I take this as an opportunity to embark on a staff development exercise with the curriculum area manager. It is the job of middle managers to ensure that the routines of the school – promptness to lessons, preparation, homework setting and marking – are being adhered to. It becomes the head teacher's responsibility when offences are so widespread that disciplinary or competency procedures need to be taken. No head teacher can expect to 'win' all of these issues. It is important to de-personalize matters and to be magnanimous in defeat or victory. It will have been a traumatic experience for a member of staff or a parent to appeal to a committee of the governing body. The member of staff will still be a professional colleague when the dust settles. There is enough negativity in the world without the head teacher adding to it!

THE EXTERNALS

The head teacher has prime responsibility for dealing with the external factors that impinge upon the life of the school. These include parents, the local community, the LEA, Office for Standards in Education (Ofsted) and the Department for Education and Employment (DfEE). The DfEE and Ofsted are working to a framework that it is difficult, if not impossible, to influence. It is a futile waste of energy to fight against the inevitability of their agendas, although one can try to be selective through prioritizing activities and policies.

Parents must be given the confidence that security, care and the opportunity to learn is provided for those whom they have entrusted to the school. Given hard work on a personal and group basis, parents can be helped to understand more clearly their part in ensuring educational success. This can be a rewarding task, but requires clarity of thought, speech and writing to couch complex educational issues in terms that parents can understand. The head teacher cannot afford to keep parental perceptions at arm's length. They are the school's best supporters, but they are rightly concerned primarily with what happens to their child. It is the head teacher's responsibility to ensure the best possible fit between individual needs and aspirations whilst keeping true to the institution's overall philosophy.

Winning the confidence of parents and dealing promptly with pupil misbehaviour builds the confidence of the community in the school. This can be helped through visiting and contributing to local community groups and by identifying those community issues that coincide with school issues. Most of all, schools have to listen to what the community has to say and then take appropriate action.

HOW WE KNOW IT'S WORKING

It is relatively straightforward for the head teacher to see the visible results of clear philosophy rigorously applied. It will be evident in the bright, frequently changed and undamaged display work on the corridors, the well-ordered corridor behaviour, the air of expectant learning in classrooms, the lack of vandal damage, and declining absence and lateness statistics.

There can be no doubt that pupils respond well to praise and schools respond well to external validation of their practices. During my headship the school gained the Schools' Curriculum Award, Technology Enhancement status, rapidly rising examination results, Healthy School status, the Paul Hamlyn award and two government Charter Marks. In an urban working-class comprehensive, the school maintained its week in France, started a series of student exchanges with our Comenius partners in Sweden, the Czech Republic, Italy and Hungary, as well as gaining funding from European sources to work with adults and the community. The feelings of self-worth that this engendered created its own momentum for improvement. As I left the school, it was awarded Investor in People status.

Being a head teacher is the most rewarding job I know. It needs clarity of thought, clarity of vision, clarity of articulation and the ability to lift everyone else when matters are at their bleakest.

Creating Colorado winners

MARY JARVIS

Since 1988 I have been principal of Smoky Hill High School in Colorado. Prior to Smoky Hill, I served for one year as an associate principal in a large St Louis suburban high school. I began my administration career in 1976 as the first female high school assistant principal in St Louis County, where I served for 11 years, finishing my doctorate in administration at Southern Illinois University. In November 1996, I became an international consultant working with administrators from the United Arab Emirates and surrounding countries.

SMOKY HILL HIGH SCHOOL

SOCIO-ECONOMIC PROFILE

The school is a public, comprehensive, suburban, college-oriented high school. There are 2941 students, 300 employees, 350 course offerings and a decentralized budget in excess of US $500,000. It is one of five in the Cherry Creek School District, Englewood, Colorado. Students come from a variety of income levels, living in homes that range from those whose value is US $500,000 to those that are no larger than 80 square metres. Some live in apartment or public subsidized housing. School enrolment stability is 94 per cent with 6.7 per cent of students receiving free or reduced price meals.

The 180-day calendar comprises two 18-week sessions. The average daily attendance rate is 93 per cent. The overall graduation rate for the 1998–99 school year was 91 per cent. White students had a graduation rate of 91.4 per cent; Hispanic 85.4 per cent; African-American 86.2 per cent; Asian/Pacific Islander 87.9 per cent; and American Indian 100 per cent.

Smoky Hill High School has received many local, state and national awards. Most prestigious is the United States Department of Education's Blue Ribbon Schools Award in 1991. For combating adolescent chemical use and abuse, Smoky Hill received the William E Simon award for exemplary programmes, one of 14 high national schools to receive the award. The key to success has remained the same: 'Small things done consistently in strategic places create major impact.'

PORTRAIT OF THE SCHOOL: 1989–2000

When it opened in 1974, Smoky Hill was designed to be unlike any school Colorado had seen before. Using the house plan, which incorporated the strengths of successful small and large schools, it attracted people who dreamed of a new era. After 26 years, dreamers both old and new remain constant in their goal which is to provide the best educational opportunities for as many students as possible. The highly personalized spirit, which drives the goal of greatness, still exists. Smoky Hill is an upbeat, caring and challenging place for students and adults.

When I arrived, the house plan and its neighbourhood concept had been abandoned. An $8 million renovation had occurred to 'close in' the houses, putting Smoky Hill High into one building. It is enormous, over 36,000 square metres, and is the largest high school under one roof in the state. I thought Smoky Hill was an unusual name and soon learned that the main hallway of the school covered the route that brought settlers to the confluence of the South Platte River and the Cherry Creek in the 1880s, the Smoky Hill Trail.

As the new principal, I quickly identified the factors that contributed to Smoky Hill's success. The local school district philosophy of site-based management energizes people. Teachers, principals and parents share greater authority to make decisions than their counterparts do nationwide. While others struggle to launch site-based strategies, Smoky Hill continues to fine tune a philosophy that has served it well. Collaborative approaches to problem-solving and decision-making, involving all possible constituencies, allow for the creation of a comprehensive academic programme. An example of this occurred shortly after the tax election failed in 1992. Department chairs, faced with fewer resources for purchasing textbooks and supplementary materials, developed a 'super-fund'. Each department agreed to give up 5 per cent of its budget and freeze it. Any budget increases due to student growth were channelled into the super-fund. At the conclusion of each school year, department chairs submitted proposals for textbooks and supplementary materials to a group of peers. Summed up by one department chair, 'it's a matter of trust'. Resources in excess of US $70,000 are distributed in a fair, equitable and collaborative process. Throughout the growth years, resources were commensurate with student growth, but beginning with the 2000–01 year the population again declines. Difficult decisions about budgetary allocations have to be shared. Decisions will always continue to be made based on 'what is best for kids'.

In 1991 I began the task of developing a shared vision statement for Smoky Hill High. A collaborative process with representatives from business, government and the school community, students, parents and teachers, created the following shared vision: 'The primary goal of Smoky Hill High School, in partnership with the community, is to provide opportunities and encouragement for the academic, social, occupational and intellectual development of each student.' To achieve this vision, our school, parents and community will foster:

- first and foremost, a stimulating and comprehensive curriculum;
- informed decision-making and involved citizenship;
- respect and appreciation for the diversity of individuals and ideas;
- experiences that develop a positive attitude toward self;
- support of environments for the explorations of a student's potential;
- associations between students and the community for mutual benefit.

The purpose of these themes was to establish the rationale around which decisions are made, change is supported and creativity encouraged, in order to make 'a good school even better'. This shared vision has been the guiding force for subsequent innovations.

Within the first years of my administrative career, the major educational challenges for the school became clear. These were caused by both internal and external pressures. An increasingly diverse and growing student population, legislative mandates and the expectation for positive public relations all made a contribution. The increasing role of information technology was also recognized. Another challenge continues to be the impact of open enrolment. The Colorado legislature passed a bill allowing students to attend any school they chose, regardless of their residential location. As long as families provide transportation and the school has space available, students move freely among and between schools and districts. Marketing Smoky Hill has become imperative in order to attract high-calibre students.

Curriculum issues relate to the upgrading of content and expectations. The International Baccalaureate programme, competency-based classes, dropping the 'D' grade, and department audits are underway or under consideration. A technology audit is currently the focus of the North Central accreditation process.

The final challenge is the 'greying' of the school. Many of the teachers who opened the school 26 years ago have retired or are nearing retirement. In 2000, five master teachers, who were also department chairs, retired. Strategies to take advantage of the chronologically gifted staff must continue, so that mentoring can flourish and new teachers can take the place of those who have served Smoky Hill for nearly three decades.

Every day a visitor can see the marching band practising on the fields or the faculty taking noon-time power walks down the community fitness trail. A physics class may be using the balcony in the hallway to conduct a demonstration. The visitor can marvel at the countless ways in which student success is celebrated in displays. Fund-raisers and community service projects will be displayed in the student activity area. Banners won by state champion academic teams decorate the halls, along with department honour rolls and the principal's honour roll, an academic hall of fame area and valedictorian photograph. There are flags from each of the countries with which the school has had foreign exchanges. The school's most cherished banner reads: 'Through these halls walk students, faculty and staff who have been recognized nationally for their outstanding attitudes and performance.' The United States Department of Education visually supports the value we place on diversity and excellence.

SIGNIFICANT CHANGES, CHALLENGES AND SOLUTIONS

Reflecting on the years as principal, I realized that the graduating class of 2000 was in first grade when I began at Smoky Hill. As they grew and developed through 12 years of education, I wondered who these young people were. From an unnamed source on the Internet I found an answer. The quotation gives a sense of the mind set and historical perspective of those high school students from across the United States who will graduate as the 'Class of 2000'.

These students were born in 1982; they have no meaningful recollection of the Reagan era and do not know that he was shot. They were pre-pubescent when the Gulf War was waged. There has been only one Pope and they can really only remember two presidents. When they were eight years old, the Berlin Wall fell. When they were 10, the Soviet Union broke apart and they do not remember the Cold War. They have never feared nuclear war and they are too young to remember the 'Challenger' spacecraft blowing up. Tianamen Square means nothing to them. Their lifetime has always included AIDS. They never had a polio shot and they likely do not know what the disease was.

This paints a startling picture of who will leave our schools in 2000. As a community, have we really changed and created new programmes, new curriculum and organizational strategies to meet the needs of a generation far different from those who graduated a decade ago? What about the influence of parents and the community as a school evolves over a 12-year time period?

In conversation with colleagues, I suggest educational leaders in the United States are constantly dealing with 'the new shareholder'. These adults, many of whom are parents, seem to be better informed. They also are more self-serving, younger and more independent. They tend to be more female, with a new independence, sometimes more irrational than rational. I have often wondered if they would like to 'take over' American public education. In discussion with parent groups, I am continually amazed at the amount of data and fact-finding capabilities they bring to the table when attempting to change policy, curriculum or organizational procedures.

Authors who write about the challenges associated with change processes have a common theme. When a leader expresses the desire to change an organization, it is often perceived as telling competent people that they are really incompetent. This single dilemma often causes leaders and organizations to fail to meet the challenge of change.

I have faced many challenges as the principal of a large suburban high school, but will focus on those that led to the greatest changes. External or internal forces, causing me to ask the question 'what needs to be done?' initiated each of these. Beginning with an enrolment of 2500 in 1989, the school saw a decline over the next two years to 2200. The enrolment than began to climb rapidly, and by 1997 Smoky Hill was at its largest with 3160 students. Two years later, we had 2941 on campus, with a prediction of approximately 2500 by 2003. With this fluctuation came many staffing eliminations, then hirings, as well as changes in the physical structure of the school, the most notable being the addition of 18 mobile classrooms. Our schedule went from an eight- to a nine-period day, with many of the older students beginning at 7.15 am and ending at 12.30 pm. The younger students begin at 9.00 am and end at 3.10 pm. The change in the schedule necessitated much co-operation from faculty, staff and the community.

A second notable change has been the heightened awareness of security issues and concerns for the safety of students in high schools across the United States. The school shootings in April 1999 at Columbine High School, Littleton, Colorado caused every school administrator to take notice. Prior to the Columbine incident, we had begun to take additional security precautions by increasing the number of campus security personnel, surveillance cameras, sophisticated two-way radios for all administrative and security staff, and the development of a school-wide safety plan with personnel training. After Columbine, security efforts doubled both psychologically and visibly.

Changes in administrative personnel over the years are significant, as nine assistant principals have served under my leadership. Many of them have gone on to be successful high school principals. Additionally, I have personally appointed over 65 per cent of the faculty which allowed me to hire talented professional teachers to lead many of the new curriculum programmes, an example being the rigorous International Baccalaureate (IB) programme that began in 1991.

The IB programme includes a two-year pre-IB and two-year IB college preparatory curriculum, which challenges the best scholars and leads to the IB diploma. In 2000 there were over 500 students in the pre-IB and IB programme, for which students receive college credit towards the IB diploma.

Smoky Hill High School has seen a significant increase in the number of advanced placement courses offered. In 1997, there were 27 advanced placement scholars, 41 in 1998 and 66 in 1999. These additions to the curriculum are intended to provide a more rigorous programme for the above-average student. Currently we have over 600 students enrolled on advanced placement courses.

Another addition to the 350 courses at Smoky Hill High School is the Advancement Via Individual Determination (AVID) programme. This programme, which began in San Diego, is nationally recognized and offers college preparatory elective programmes for students 'in the middle' who have the potential to succeed in higher education. Often these students come from under-represented groups, and many of them will be the first generation in their family to attend a college or university. AVID lessons focus on study skills and library research to help students succeed in English, mathematics, science, history and foreign languages.

PRESENT STATE OF SCHOOL

The students are terrific and the key ingredient in the school's success. The graduation rate has consistently been above 90 per cent and standardized test scores exceed state and national norms. The school has been the home to both Hispanic scholars and national merit achievement finalists. Seventy-five per cent of Smoky Hill's students are college bound and most take more classes than are required. Many successfully balance work, athletics and activities with their academic studies. Others have demanding family responsibilities. Whatever their situations, students display a loyalty to the 'red and green' and to their mascot, the buffalo. The undefinable bromide 'school spirit' exists in plenty.

The faculty is outstanding. More than 75 per cent have a Master's degree or above. The staff designs and implements the curriculum, constructs the instructional budget and utilizes innovative, creative teaching strategies. Faculty members are highly visible, spending many hours supporting activities, athletics and other programmes.

Parents are welcomed and encouraged to become actively involved. The accountability committee, after-prom party, various support groups and parent ambassadors are all valued. The latter are parent volunteers who have walked the halls to help keep the school safe since the Columbine tragedy.

The best means of capturing the essence of Smoky Hill High School at the start of a new century is to describe the difference which school life makes to the daily lives of students. To illustrate the essence of caring attitudes, the value of personalizing the high school will be described and examples given of successful programmes.

As the school moves into the 21st century, personalizing the environment must remain as constant as high academic expectations and the belief that all kids can succeed (Jarvis, 1996). As principal, how am I able to do this in a large suburban high school? I need to take the reader back 36 years to the time when I was a student in a large suburban high school and was anything but a model member of the class of 1966. It was during my sophomore year that a teacher reached out and made a difference in my life, literally turning my life around. It was a gift. From the experience, I knew my mission in life would be to give back that same gift to students and to model for faculty, staff and students the ability to put caring relationships and support first on each day's agenda. This has significantly changed the climate of Smoky Hill to a place that truly cares about people.

In the new Carnegie and National Association of Secondary School Principals (NASSP) report, *Breaking Ranks: Changing an American Institution* (1996), personalization emerges as one of the six main themes for high schools to consider as they move into the 21st century. The report suggests that high schools must break into units of no more than 600 students, so that teachers and students can get to know each other better. Teachers should use a variety of instructional strategies that accommodate individual learning styles and engage students, every student should have a personal adult advocate and a personal plan for progress. At Smoky Hill many opportunities exist for students to have a personal advocate, and programmes are in place to assist students who have special academic needs. Two successful schemes illustrate the 'personal plan' approach.

Probably the most powerful and effective scheme at Smoky Hill is the adopt-a-senior programme. This matches at-risk seniors with adult mentors in the hope that, when 'senioritis' sets in, someone will be there to help and encourage the senior to graduate on time. Seniors must be willing to recognize social and emotional problems that might preclude graduation, be committed to graduating and be willing to meet with a mentor regularly. Volunteers who are willing to act as mentor for one to five seniors are solicited from the faculty and staff. The volunteers make introductory contact with parents by telephone, commit themselves to frequent contact with students and collect monthly progress reports. Selected participants sign up with a mentor of their choice. Interactions are individually arranged to meet the needs of the senior, monthly progress reports are collected and periodic meetings are offered for mentors. School-wide data suggests that the scheme makes the strongest contribution to the increase in the graduation rate at the school.

Smoky Hill also attempts to help ninth graders (14- to 15-year-olds), in particular those who are struggling academically, to build a foundation for success through an immersion programme. This gives those assessed as deficient in both language and mathematics an opportunity to improve their skills to at least a basic level. Immersion is designed to focus on basic English, study skills, basic mathematics and academic support time, a time when students have an opportunity to complete their homework during the school day with help from a teacher. To gain entrance to the immersion programme, eighth-grade students are recommended by teachers, counsellors and deans at the middle-level feeder schools. Class size is kept small, 15 to 20 students, in order to promote intensified work. Students have an opportunity to venture out of the immersion programme to take classes in physical education, computer science, art, music or other electives, but they do not usually take a social studies or science class in the first year.

Immersion is overwhelmingly successful. Students who participated in the first year turned multiple D and F report cards into A, B, and C grades at the end of their first semester. Comments from the student's eighth-grade teachers used phrases such as 'shows no interest in class', 'does not complete assignments in a timely manner', 'often is uncooperative'. Report cards at the end of the ninth-grade first semester included comments such as 'positive attitude', 'shows strong effort', 'excellent conduct', 'assumes responsibility' and 'good class participation'.

Probably the most powerful testimony for the immersion programme comes from the students themselves. A questionnaire was administered at the end of the first year and student comments included: 'At first the idea of coming to the high school was scary, mostly because I was new and wasn't prepared. I already had people telling me I was a potential dropout. But now moving on is exciting and if a teacher asks me a question I don't cringe in my desk. I have more room for learning and less for worries.' With a little help and a smaller group setting, students are able to master basic skills and have a better chance to graduate.

In such a large school, the above programmes cannot begin to meet all needs. A range of strategies to personalize the school is needed. Teachers take five classes on a nine-period day and students are required to take six. The school is an open campus and students come and go at will, often leaving for lunch with friends. Both teachers and students maximize the use of the flexibility and openness of this schedule, which enables students to connect regularly with adults who support them. Whether it be a one-to-one help session, as part of the adopt-a-senior or immersion programmes, or just an opportunity for students and teachers to sit down and talk about what's good and bad, the flexible schedule allows adults and students to connect beyond the classroom setting on a regular basis.

At the community celebration of my award as 1996 NASSP/MetLife National Principal of the Year, I had the opportunity to visit the teacher who made such a difference to my life 36 years ago. Gail Mullen Rickard was on hand to help celebrate the success that she so generously influenced: 'Thank you, Mary, for telling me how much I influenced your life,' Gail said. 'As a teacher, you never know when you make a difference. You might not know it for another 36 years.'

Someone once said: 'A hundred years from now it will not matter what my bank account was, the sort of house I lived in, or the kind of car I drove. But the world may be different because I was important in the life of a young person.' As a professional educator, one must never lose sight of that simple belief.

PRINCIPAL'S STYLE AND APPROACH

As I reflect upon my personal growth as a leader and the many changes that have occurred at Smoky Hill High School in 12 years, I am reminded of writings from

Roy Rowan (1996), author of *Powerful People*. He was a journalist who spent 50 years covering the world's greatest events and interviewing some very powerful people, including Marshal Tito, Douglas McArthur and Mao Zedong. He found four leader attributes that have resonated with me as I approached necessary changes in curriculum and organization management: 'stay focused and enthusiastic; timing is everything; when you act, do so with vigour; don't take rejection personally'. Through the challenges of administrative life, I have tried to remember these positive leader behaviours.

Additionally, I would encourage readers to become familiar with the writings of Meg Wheatley, author of *Leadership and the New Science* and *A Simpler Way*. Wheatley often talks about leaders maintaining a sense of possibility. The role of a true leader is to hold a space open for others to emerge. The path of leadership is one of courage and sacrifice and we must create environments where we can express our own clarity of voice no matter what the topic (Wheatley, 1992). She states, 'the major issue facing us is not the wide gap between those with resources and those without, it is the wide gap between those who believe in possibilities and those who do not' (Wheatley, 1992: 26). As a leader, what is really possible for your organization? What do you really believe in, regardless of resources made available? What are your passions?

In 1991, Smoky Hill applied for the United States Department of Education's Blue Ribbon excellence award. Winning the Blue Ribbon was one of my early passions. In the written application the faculty and staff were asked: 'How does the principal inspire staff, parents, and students to accomplish the school's mission?' The answer was as follows:

> Principal Dr Mary Jarvis focuses the energies of the many constituencies by modelling, reinforcing, and promoting the shared vision. In class meetings with students, in faculty cluster meetings, in weekly contact with the Parent Teacher Community Organization (PTCO) president, in her always-open office, she stimulates, congeals and looks ahead. Her development of a high level of trust and her tolerance for differences serve to release the energies of her staff. Dr Mary Jarvis' style is characterized by saying 'yes' more often than 'no', and lending unequivocal support for risk-taking and new ideas. Her style of leadership creates a collaborative problem-solving approach that utilizes the talents of assistant principals, department chairpersons, faculty, students and parents.

Perhaps my leadership style is best described by looking at the signs that hang in my office, clearly visible to all those who join me for conversation or present me with a problem. The first is a simple sign with two columns:

leadership

this	not this
cheerleader	cop
enthusiast	referee
nurturer	devil's advocate
coach	nay-sayer
facilitator	pronouncer

Other signs in my office are:

- WE ARE IN THE BUSINESS OF CREATING WINNERS, AND NOT PICKING THEM.
- LIVE IN TODAY, I DO.
- SEE EVERYTHING, OVERLOOK A GREAT DEAL AND IMPROVE A LITTLE AT A TIME.

Last, but not least, is my guiding philosophy of leadership: 'Small things done consistently in strategic places create major impact.' Over the 24 years I have been in secondary school administration, I have modified my leadership style, but seldom have I strayed from the values conveyed in these messages.

A profound and influential article on leadership was written in 1974 by Robert Starrat. He wrote:

> Leadership is a sometimes thing. Sometimes, because what is described as appropriate leadership behaviour in one setting is not appropriate in another; sometimes, because some circumstances will not tolerate leadership behaviour; sometimes, because new ideas and new insights which are described as essential to leadership behaviour do not happen every day or even once a month; sometimes, because luck and mischievous human whimsy play such a large part in achieving results that might mistakenly be attributed to leadership behaviour... A leader is one who is profoundly convinced of the significance of what he and his group are doing and communicates this verbally and non-verbally to those inside and outside the organization. The leader is a visionary, a person who senses a dramatic urgency in the task that he and his followers face, or who sees a beauty, a dignity or a depth to the task and to the processes of accomplishing the task. He has a sense he is actually playing a part in history.

I have never lost sight of the wisdom and the style of leadership described by Robert Starrat and I attempt to communicate his message every day. In addition, I have realized that there are three key factors for effective leadership behaviour: roles, responsibilities and relationships (Jarvis and Chavez, 1997). The awareness of our role as leader goes beyond the typical description associated with administration.

Leaders must not only understand, but also welcome, a new reality that calls for a variety of roles. Needs and expectations of the public have fundamentally changed the role of administrators. The thinking of leaders must shift in order that their roles include: creator of context, seeker of information, initiator of communications, promoter of possibilities and guardians of morale (Jarvis and Chavez, 1997: 35).

'Creating context' means sharing the big picture with the school and its community; sharing the political, economic and social shifts that influence the educational enterprise. It means serving as facilitator, negotiator and persuader in order to create the right settings for people to have important conversations. In this sense, leaders orchestrate multiple beliefs, values and expectations in order to define the fundamental mission of the organization.

Often leaders view their role as a giver of information. The changing role is that of a 'seeker of information'. Communities are dynamic and leaders must assume they do not know all of what their constituents want, value and expect. Stephen Covey, author of *The Seven Habits of Highly Effective People* (1989: 235), challenges us to 'seek first to understand'. This is contrary to the usual practice of 'seek first to tell'. By virtue of being a seeker of information, leaders see themselves as active listeners. This means genuinely wanting to comprehend the issues from the viewpoint of others. It means to absorb the context of others' emotions and passions. Seekers have no choice but to go this extra mile (Covey, 1989: 36).

Serving as 'initiators of communication' means anticipating and illuminating the issues because it is the right thing to do. While problems of student motivation and behaviour, poor test scores, budget shortfalls and philosophical differences persist in education, they are not the private property of administrators. We need to articulate the issues and engage the larger community in possible solutions. In this way confidence and trust are established.

A leader as 'promoter of possibilities' is critical if genuine change is to take place. Without leaders in this role, the public will pry open the doors of change. To serve as promoter of possibilities, leaders must demonstrate risk-taking by thoughtfully supporting employee initiatives and by advocating ideas that are valued by the community. Not all proposals put forward by the community are aligned with the beliefs and values of their appointed or elected leaders. The challenge is to reconcile this reality and then take action. Leadership is action, not position.

Educators are in a highly intensive human relations business. The role of leader as 'guardian of morale' is critical to success. 'People don't care how much you know until they know how much you care.' It is true that you cannot legislate the heart and so, to implement new programmes and services, leaders must enhance the capacity of employees to carry out new decisions. Leaders must model optimism and enthusiasm to have a direct impact on the morale of others.

Using these roles, the following responsibilities can help leaders to attain greater success. Ensure clarity in the mission and guiding principles of the organization. Recruit, retain and reward people whose sole passion relates to human development, their own, students and colleagues. Walk the talk. Model thinking and behaviours that are desirable in others. Exhibit a sense of curiosity and an availability to learn and adapt. Serve as keeper of the dream through organizational story telling. Be vulnerable. Teach what you know and say what you don't know. Anticipate, illuminate and respond to criticism. Foster celebrations of people and successful outcomes. Give credit where it is due. Tell the truth. Empower others to seek solutions. Mentor unselfishly. Model trusting behaviours. Be visible and approachable. Demonstrate accountability. Communicate, communicate, communicate. (Wheatley, 1992: 37).

Leaders must make sense of conflicting responsibilities and maintain a realistic balance. I have struggled many times to maintain the balance between, according to McCall *et al* (1988: 144):

> acting alone and working with others. Making tough decisions and treating people with compassion. Having the confidence to act and the humility to know there are other views. Seizing opportunities and planning for the future. Taking control and accepting the inevitable. Persevering in the face of adversity, yet changing direction when you're wrong.

The leadership style that allows balance to occur, thus promoting win–win situations, has relationships at its core. People make things happen. People bring life to visions, missions and purpose. Investment in relationships is an investment in the achievement of goals. Nowhere is this truer than in the relationships between teachers and students. When the relationship is positive, constructive and mutually respectful, the opportunity for learning is enhanced.

It is also true for adults. When leaders foster relationships between and among teachers, parents and community members, a synergy occurs. During a presentation, Stephen Covey elaborated on the concept of synergy and stated:

> Synergy is creatively producing better solutions than those we could have produced independently. This requires deep empathic listening and great courage in expressing perspectives and opinions in ways that show respect for the other person's view. Out of that genuine interaction come insights that are truly synergistic.

When synergy is evident, not only is productivity high, but the relationships are characterized as having the quality of a covenant, helping people to deal more effectively with conflict and change. All too often, relationships are contractual in nature. They are based on formal agreements. Leaders must invest in covenant relationships for the highest good to be achieved. The leadership team at Smoky Hill High School operates from a covenant, reviewed regularly in regard to how business is conducted and how people are treated. Our covenant has had a powerful impact on the team, individually as well as collectively.

A leader never achieves success alone. The most important factor in organizational success is people. Effective leaders unlock potential and creativity through challenge, empowerment, and encouragement. For truly successful leadership, a focus on roles, responsibilities and relationships is the key. The accompanying concepts provide a springboard for reflection and dialogue. This helps leaders to define purpose, both personal and organizational, and to identify actions that foster achievement and seek greater meaning in the work itself. (Jarvis and Chavez, 1997: 37)

In conclusion, I list my '12 pearls of wisdom', in the hope they may be helpful in facing the everyday challenges of school leadership.

- People first, programme second.
- Treat children like adults, adults like children.
- Encourage 'possibility thinking'.
- The only way to lose is to try to win.
- Knowledge is power, sharing knowledge is more powerful.
- Fake it.
- Trust our own intuition, but doubt our own wisdom.
- Just for today, judge no one.
- Don't expect anyone to care like you do.
- Beware of gift givers.
- SWTQ (Sit With The Question).
- Do something with the gaps, the gaps between common sense and common practice.

REFERENCES

Covey, S (1989) *The Seven Habits of Highly Effective People*, Simon and Schuster, New York

Jarvis, M (1996) Incentives to Succeed: Personalizing the high school, *The High School Magazine*, **3** (4), pp12–17

Jarvis, M and Chavez, C (1997) The Three R's of Leadership, *The Phi Kappa Phi Journal,* **77** (1), pp35–37

McCall, M Hombardo, M and Morrison, A (1988) *The Lessons of Experience*, Lexington Books, New York

National Association of Secondary School Principals (1996) *Breaking Ranks: Changing an American institution*, NASSP, Reston, Virginia

Rowan, R (1996) *From Mayo to Now: A reporter's fifty-two year pursuit of powerful people*, Carroll & Graf Publications, New York

Starrat, R (1974) Contemporary Talk on Leadership: Too many kings in the parade? *Notre Dame Journal of Education*, **18**, pp5–14

Wheatley, M (1992) *Leadership and the New Science*, Berrett-Kochler, San Francisco

Wheatley, M and Kellner-Rogers, M (1996) *A Simpler Way*, Berrett-Koehler, San Francisco

Primary focus

MICHAEL PRITCHARD

Looking back, I suppose it is not surprising that I found myself working as a head teacher within the world of education. Yet, on leaving school, I did not consider working with children. No, I wanted to be either in the army or a policeman. I suppose that becoming a military policeman for three years indicated a non-confrontational style of leadership. It was not a decision over which I took a great deal of time; it just seemed that it was the right thing to do. On leaving the army I joined the Northumberland Constabulary. Again, it seemed natural to continue working at something I enjoyed. At this time I married my wife Pamela, who was already an enthusiastic teacher in a middle school. As I plodded the beat at night, and drove 'panda' cars round the streets of Whitley Bay, I began to question why I was physically exhausted at the end of a shift and yet not mentally stretched at all. My wife, on the other hand, seemed to be just as busy as me but she had that something extra, a total commitment to planning exciting and challenging activities for children. Wherever we went, she would see opportunities for learning and for gathering resources. She even displayed enthusiasm and joy in doing so. Our friends, most of whom were teachers, also shared a common language, lifestyle and vitality that I, as a policeman, simply did not have. And so, four years at Newcastle College of Education qualified me to embark on my chosen career. It was then that I looked back and joined my two brothers, my sister-in-law, my mother and my grandfather. All of them had chosen teaching as their profession. Hardly surprising really that the odds were very much in favour of Michael Pritchard becoming a teacher.

I believe that it takes about five years of teaching to be able to become fully qualified. For the first year I asked myself, 'Can I teach?' I was planning from day to day, and surviving the challenges of the Christmas concert, parties, open evenings, educational visits and report writing. I use the word survive deliberately, as it reflects the context of anyone new joining an established organization. Staff, parents and children all know the structure of the school, its routines and organization. For the new teacher, and the new head there has to be a willingness to learn, an understanding that mistakes will be made, and a desire and determination to improve. By the end of my first year a chapter in my life closed and I was fired with excitement and enthusiasm to continue the book the following September. I began again with a new class of children, building on my first-hand learning experiences from the previous year. Next comes, 'How do I teach?' This stage develops into trying different strategies, building on successful outcomes and discarding those that do not work. Four years later, having moved to a private boys' school, I asked the philosophical question, 'Why am I teaching?' I was then able to be my own mentor, appraiser and critic. This process was repeated when later I was appointed to my present headship.

Curriculum leadership, involvement in extra-curricular activities and becoming a school governor were challenges that I readily accepted and enjoyed. I discovered that I loved the job. My career moved through teaching a class of infant children for two years, about which a whole book could be written, becoming an advisory teacher for science and technology, a deputy head and finally, where I am today, a head of a primary school in Durham. As an advisory teacher, I visited nearly all 88 schools in Gateshead. I discovered that leadership styles were different in every school, but the one common thread seemed to be that the head teacher was responsible for the school. Visiting schools for short periods of time, I discovered the 'stale cabbage curriculum'. By this I mean that just as you can make immediate judgements about a kitchen if there is a pervading smell of stale cabbage, so too it is possible to 'smell' the curriculum within a school. No matter how old or new the building, age or deprivation of the children within, in a good school there is a positive ethos, an attractive environment and sounds of happy children that can be detected throughout the building. I learned quickly from these visits and tried to build up a global picture of all the positive features that were in evidence in a school where children learned positively and staff seemed to enjoy their work. As deputy head for just one year I was challenged to put into practice my learning and discovered another truth about leadership, namely that improvement is best effected from within the classroom. As a full time teacher of 8- to 11-year-olds I discovered the need for the deputy head to listen to views and to temper them when meeting with the head teacher. Management decisions from the head to me were always carried out after I had been given the opportunity to discuss them with her. Those were difficult days in primary education. The National Curriculum was in its infancy and the primary school world was darting about trying to make a success of schemes of work that were later to be found inappropriate. Never was there a better time to illustrate the truth behind the saying that, whilst all improvement requires change, changes do not always lead to improvement. After 13 years of teaching, I was appointed as head teacher to my present school, Langley Moor Primary.

LANGLEY MOOR PRIMARY SCHOOL

THE SCHOOL'S CONTEXT

Langley Moor is 3 kilometres outside Durham City and has its roots in a mining community. The school was opened in 1887 and catered for miners' children. Throughout the first half of the 20th century it was used for the education of children in the village. During the 1950s, two new towns, Washington and Newton Aycliffe, were developed and all the villages in Durham were categorized by government. Langley Moor was a category D village, which meant that no housing development of any sort was allowed. The thinking behind this move was to encourage people to move to the New Towns. As a result, Langley Moor declined in population and the numbers attending the school fell. The adjoining infant school was demolished and the junior school was renamed as primary. However, the new towns became full at the end of the 1970s and the category D was lifted, allowing for expansion in Langley Moor and the surrounding villages. They grew and merged into an extension of Durham city. Housing development began, providing attractive homes for the first-time buyer. Council house accommodation was sold or taken over by housing trusts. The parent population changed from being either unemployed or working class to aspiring white-collar workers. Today the parents mostly own their own homes, are in employment, many with both mother and father working, and present as 'average' families with about 2.2 children! There are few professional parents, but all are supportive of the school and want a better education for their children. About 17 per cent of the parents claim free school meals for their children.

INTO HEADSHIP

When I began my headship, there were 130 children with five teachers in mixed-age classes, from a reception group of five-year-olds to eleven-year-olds in Year 6. The National Curriculum was being implemented, teacher appraisal was in its infancy and the testing of seven-year-olds had just begun. For the previous two years, the school's head teacher had been on secondment and had just been appointed to a permanent post with the Local Education authority (LEA) as a staff tutor. The school had been led by the deputy head who did not apply for the headship. At interview I told the governors of my vision for education and proposed specific directions for their school. I outlined honestly my philosophy, told them what needed to be done and what I would do if they chose me. So, when they appointed me, I felt a great deal of support and trust from the governors and was confident to begin carrying out my role in line with my thinking.

Members of staff were all keen and enthusiastic, knowing that change was needed. Local management of the school was due to begin the following year and it appeared that all eyes were looking at me to take them forward. And why not? After all, this is what I had said I would do at interview. I regarded it as my job. During discussions with the staff it became apparent that my philosophical ideas for education were in line with theirs. In particular, one member of staff, a senior teacher, shared my child-centred approach to education. My first few weeks involved me in visiting all the staff in their classrooms, sharing the learning experience with them and talking informally after school about their teaching background, present position and hopes for the future. I did not attempt any formal appraisal at this stage. It was far too early. I gave a listening ear and was able to build up a picture of their strengths. I felt sure that any weaknesses or problems staff had would have come out at this early stage and, encountering none, I was able to turn to other matters.

I began by carrying out an audit of the areas of school life: children, staff, parents, governors, curriculum and building. There were adequate systems in place to ensure that no one area of the school was seriously weak and so I decided, using the notion that I could change the building quicker than I could people, to make changes to the building. The primary child and teacher spend nearly all of their day in a single room, making the classroom their home. I saw 'county-style' decoration throughout the school, with colour combinations in every room of battleship greys and blues and the odd tint of a 'weak green'. Several storerooms were full of nativity costumes, old mouse-eaten hymn books and other resources that had been used once and put away. A local scrap merchant came and cleared these rooms at no charge to us on the understanding that he could sell for scrap anything he could salvage. It took three men three days to clear the rooms, corridor and hall.

Then, with the help of parents and staff, we set about decorating the non-teaching areas of the school. Everyone noticed the difference and gave it a welcome. It is worth mentioning that I did not attempt to circumvent the LEA rules and regulations regarding building maintenance, neither did I suggest to the staff that they should help. Rather, by starting the work myself, I found that others offered their services. This 'hands-on' management approach was my style of working. In any situation we must recognize our strengths and use them to the full. Parents began to comment on the change in the appearance of the school. It really was beginning to look a great deal better and I was determined to set a timescale for the redecoration of the whole of the school within a three-year period.

MAKING PLANS

A key tool in my leadership role was the school management plan. Initially regarded as a document for planning for the next five years, it soon became apparent that, with the swiftness of change in the primary curriculum and the looming of school inspection, the most that I could hope for was a detailed one-year plan and a skeleton three-year projection. Curriculum co-ordinators were appointed. As there were only six of us, this meant that whilst all had more than one area, some had four. Priorities for the development of curriculum areas were agreed at staff meetings and a development plan was incorporated into the management plan. The LEA placed great emphasis on the school management plan. By making sure that my targets for development were clearly set out, with achievable aims and realistic timescales, I was able to filter the constant demands from different external departments to produce documentation or introduce curriculum initiatives that were not within our planned area for development. I had to be aware of the changing legal requirements and these were incorporated into the plan as the year progressed. Thus my management plan is never a definitive, complete document. It is always available and kept up to date.

It has always seemed to me that it is better to work with an organization, rather than trying to steer the great bureaucratic machine in a different direction. Therefore the delegation of funding for us was a very rewarding exercise. A suitable place for the associated hardware had to be chosen. As this was fully funded, I chose one of the storerooms in school that had no electricity, no heating, a rotten floor and no security. Central funding was found to refurbish this room into an office and at the same time I chose to refurbish the adjacent storeroom as the head teacher's office. I was thus able to tap into the major development, funded from outside resources, to provide a necessary school improvement at minimal expense.

The knock-on effect of this change released two other rooms in school previously used as offices to allow for a better staff room and library. Two further examples may help to illustrate this approach. Firstly, not long into my headship staff appraisal was making its impact. When it was my turn to be appraised by a colleague head and inspector I chose the work with my management team as the focus. I had found that in a school of six staff some observers would regard the notion of a management team as a grey area. Surely there was no need for a team! However, by using the appraisal process and involving a fellow head, the staff developed a clearer understanding of the role and function of management. Since then, I have been able to share my thoughts with senior colleagues and listen to their informed opinions knowing that other staff regard them as credible and informed professionals.

Secondly, the parent of a child suffering from cerebral palsy approached me for his admission to the reception class. I had no experience of working with physically handicapped children in a mainstream school, but as the school is a single-storey site and presented no access problems, it seemed an avenue worth investigating. I discovered that, by working with the special needs section at county hall and expecting their full support, areas of education hitherto unknown to me were opened. Suddenly physiotherapists and occupational therapists appeared and we were given a full time support assistant for the child. The support assistant meant an increase in our staffing and provided an extra body to share in the staff responsibilities. Word of our willingness to take children with special needs quickly spread and numbers increased. Everyone has gained from this venture, children and their parents, staff, and the LEA.

PROBLEMS AND RISKS

There is undoubtedly an element of risk-taking in my style of leadership but those that I do take are calculated, shared and agreed with others. I regard myself as a lateral thinker and loved tackling logic puzzles as a child. Life can be full of problems if we let them in and so an alternative approach is needed. The solution starts with a question: 'Is there a problem?' The answer is a simple yes or no. If yes, then I ask, 'Is that problem mine?' If the problem is not mine then I leave it alone and get on with other matters. If the problem is mine, I take action. Quite often people concern themselves with problems that are simply not theirs.

By the end of my first year at Langley Moor, I could see a problem looming. There was an increase in young families moving into the area and the school would need to expand. I predicted that a new teacher would have to be appointed to keep the class sizes manageable. New children would bring more revenue to the school, but that had to be balanced with the constraints concerning the physical capacity of the school. The risk was financial. There were sufficient funds for a new teacher for one year providing that we were careful in our use of resources. However, intake numbers would have to rise significantly the following year to continue employing the extra member of staff. Careful consultation with the governors and staff, outlining all the advantages and disadvantages, gained their agreement in principle. The newly qualified teacher was appointed for the next year. The benefits of increased staffing were immediately clear to all. Classes were smaller and staff responsibilities were shared between seven instead of six. Parents and governors could see the school progressing positively. When, at a later date, the school moved to seven classes, the risks were once again calculated, shared and taken.

LEADERSHIP STYLE

I once worked for a head teacher in a large private school who welcomed me on to the staff by saying: 'The door to my office is always open, but no one comes in.' This was not entirely true, but in my seven years at the school I only had occasion to enter his office twice. I learnt from that and I make myself available to staff when they need me. It is for the head teacher to provide the structure and context to enable staff to work with their children uninterrupted during the day. However, at the close of school and before we start I make sure that I am in a position to listen if needed. Routine matters are dealt with through the structure of the management team, curriculum and weekly staff meetings.

Staff development is built into my monitoring role, but I do try to respond to the human side of teaching. Delegation of responsibility to school level allowed the governors to give me the authority to respond to personal and family needs of staff. I provide teaching cover for members of staff who need time out of class during the school day and I have found that this is not abused. With having young staff, it is very rewarding for me to share with them their maturity as they move from university life into the world of the adult. Because there are only seven staff, I am able to take an interest in them as people. They respond accordingly, showing an enthusiastic commitment to the life of the school. I plan the school in-service training programme from a two-sided approach. School need is determined and staff trained accordingly. In addition personal professional development is encouraged. This can be a two-edged sword, as professional development is certainly of great benefit to the school in general, but also leads to staff becoming better equipped to fulfil roles of responsibility when promoted to other schools. It seems strange to me that in education the promotion of staff to other schools is regarded as an indicator of a manager's success, whereas in business the manager attempts at all costs to keep the able worker within the company.

The management of children is directly linked to the management of all the other aspects of school life. The learning of children, their performance, attendance, social development and self-esteem are all influenced in some degree by the school they attend. They spend a relatively short time of their life at school and yet we in education seem to have been given the responsibility for ensuring the moral behaviour of all. I remember taking my first parents' evenings many years ago. I followed the accepted practice of almost apologizing to the parents if the child could not read, despite me having worked with them during my lunch breaks and after school. Now I feel, whilst we accept that the job of the teacher is to teach, the job of the child is to learn. Putting this idea into practice, I take a great deal of time to let the children know what their job is and, of course, to let them know how well they are doing. The child has to know how to behave and what is expected. If we present clear, fair guidelines for behaviour, work and attendance, then we can expect the child to succeed. This does not result in long lists of rules displayed about the building, but rather four or five well-chosen statements that can be related to the whole of the school day. These statements are not only agreed by the staff and children in each class, but are accepted as uniform among all the children in the school. I delegate responsibility for the management of children outside the classroom to my key stage co-ordinators who, as part of the management team, are given responsibility posts.

Children are managed in their learning by the class teacher who sets attainment targets for each child at the start of the year. These targets, discussed with the previous year's teacher, are then agreed with me. Subsequently the teacher and child move through the year, hopefully reaching the set targets. End-of-year tests record achievement and provide the criteria against which the individual targets can be measured. Initially it was difficult for the staff to accept the process of target setting, but now it is seen as a positive way of measuring learning outcomes. Used as judgement criteria, colleagues now have a statistical document that records their success in the classroom. The children also respond to the challenge of clear targets for learning. They know what they have to do and can work steadily to achieve the result. Providing this process is kept at the level of the individual child, then both the child with learning difficulties, and the more able child can be challenged effectively.

Parents, from whatever background, need to be kept fully informed about what the school is doing as they are the customers. Regular open evenings to discuss their child's progress with the class teacher are held and I always make myself available if requested. My approach is to listen very carefully to the parent's concerns and never dismiss them out of hand. What may seem to be trivial to me, having an overview of the school, may be very challenging to the parent of the child concerned. Class teachers are encouraged to deal with the day-to-day concerns as often they have a better understanding of the situation. They are invariably the people who can do something about it. I join the parents on the yard at the start and finish of the school day as this gives me a sounding of 'school-yard' gossip. There are times when I choose not to be there, but these fortunately are rare. Giving the children the right message to take home can prevent many misunderstandings. Staff are encouraged to share with the children the day's learning, explaining to them what they have been doing and why. Too often the parents of reception children think they play all day!

It is easy to react immediately to a parent but it is often a mistake. It is all too easy to listen and agree with someone, change procedures to accommodate that person's views only to discover that they were a single voice and unrepresentative of the majority. Time to think, with a promise to let the parent know what has been done, allows concerns to be shared with staff who often can paint the fuller picture and provide a clearer context. Just as we have special needs children in school, we have special needs parents who have to be treated accordingly. We must understand that some parents will always have something to say about whatever has happened. Just as we need to give extra time to the child who has special needs, so too must we provide time for our special needs parents.

The ever-increasing role of the school governor has accentuated the need for the relationship between governor and head teacher to be positive and supportive. Governors are after all the controlling authority of a school. They come with a rich variety of life's experiences, few of which are from the professional context of education. I keep my chair of governors fully informed about school life and decisions that have been made, particularly those which are important or about which they would want to know. The standard of putting myself in their role and asking myself if I would want to know is a useful check in this respect. A simple telephone call is often all that is needed to give them an update of events that have occurred. Formal meetings give me the opportunity to report on school matters but also to show the way ahead, suggesting alternatives if needed. Governors have a decision-making role and I feel it is necessary to give them as clear a picture as possible to facilitate that role. They are encouraged to visit the school and I make my time available to them when they do so. They share my vision and I consider their suggestions seriously. We find that invariably we have a common understanding of both the problem and the solution. They are reassuring in their support because it was they who appointed me and I am conscious of their role in the management of the school.

In 2000 a new system of performance management was introduced together with the requirement to assess teachers for a possible additional salary – payment – yet two more changes that head teachers have to manage. A Director of Education, when asked by head teachers at meetings how they could possibly carry out all that was required of them or make their budgets meet every eventuality, always replied: 'It's your job to manage.' I hear those words reflected in what I now say to the children: 'It's your job to learn.' Head teachers today do have to lead and manage if they and their school are to be successful. Possibly the best head teacher is one who does not have a particular style that is applied to all situations, but rather an understanding that different approaches are needed to respond to different aspects of leadership. The school has seven single-age classes with a cheerful and hard-working staff who provide a happy learning environment for all the children. It is my second home and every day I look forward to arriving there. On return to my own home at the end of the day I reflect on the ever-changing nature of my job. Ultimately I need to have the ability to stand back, to put decisions into context and to trust in the support of those who understand why we are there. All these are vital qualities if individual children are to benefit.

Tackling underachievement: valuing success

MICHAEL DOIG

I have taught in five Scottish comprehensive secondary schools, beginning as a teacher of modern foreign languages in 1972 at Douglas Academy, Milngavie, Glasgow. In 1975 I moved to Shawlands Academy in Glasgow as assistant principal teacher of modern languages, becoming a principal teacher and head of modern languages at Cumbernauld High School in the following year. After five years I moved to Hermitage Academy, Helensburgh, as assistant head and four years later became depute (deputy) head at Kirkintilloch High School. In 1992 I returned to Cumbernauld as head teacher.

In recent years I have been an active member of the Headteachers' Association of Scotland (HAS) and have served as an executive member and editor of *Scottish Headlines*, the journal of HAS. Wider contributions to the teaching of modern languages have included serving as chair of the modern languages reference group for 'Higher Still', the post-16 curriculum reform in Scotland and as a member of a ministerial action group for languages.

CUMBERNAULD HIGH SCHOOL

SOCIO-ECONOMIC CONTEXT

The school is one of five comprehensive secondary schools in Cumbernauld, a New Town in central Scotland of over 50,000 inhabitants. The school was the first in the town and has a current roll of 878. It serves a wide catchment area in the centre and north of Cumbernauld. The town itself is relatively prosperous, having a good spread of businesses and small industries, as well as being home to the Inland Revenue accounts office for Scotland and a large factory owned by OKI which manufactures printers.

However, the area in the immediate vicinity of the school comprises ageing 1960s council housing stock of deteriorating quality and is largely populated by families entitled to state benefits and allowances. Free school meals are available to 28 per cent of the pupils and 38 per cent are entitled to a local authority bursary for footwear and clothing. This level of deprivation is greater than any of the other secondary schools in the town. In recent years this has been recognized by an allocation of 1.5 extra teachers to help us cope with the problems associated with social deprivation.

Despite this, the school has flourished over the years and enjoys a sound reputation. We have a significant number of pupils each year from outside our immediate catchment area, whose parents choose the school for their child. A unit for young people with communication disorders on the autistic spectrum was established in 1995 and has grown successfully ever since. Its pupils achieve an increasing amount of integration with their peer group. In January 1999 we achieved the Investors in People (IIP) award, one of a small number of Scottish secondary schools to attain this standard.

PORTRAIT OF THE SCHOOL

When I was appointed in 1992, the roll was 701 and the school was struggling to attract its expected intake. A recent inspection by Her Majesty's Inspectors of Schools (HMI) had found some deficiencies in the management of the school and of the curriculum. It provided a clear agenda for an incoming head! Some leaders of subject departments had been criticized for not monitoring curriculum and teaching. Insufficient attention had been paid to academic results.

Many staff were experienced teachers, who had given many years of loyal service to the school. Nevertheless, it was clear that there was an urgent need for fresh faces and I was fortunate that I was one of eight new staff who joined the school that year. Whilst this alone made only a small impact, it did allow me from the beginning to set a fresh agenda that I hoped would restore the fortunes of the school and reverse the decline of previous years. Of equal importance was the need to win back parents of pupils who had not chosen Cumbernauld High, preferring one of the neighbouring schools. An important plank of this approach was to target our associated primary schools. This was done by visiting each one several times and compiling a visual presentation for parents and pupils that highlighted the best aspects of Cumbernauld High.

In my previous post I had experience of helping to reverse a serious drift of pupils to a nearby school and I was determined to present my new school on its own merits. These included a focus on some very traditional aspects. For example, we were, and continue to be, one of the few schools offering Latin and rugby (not football) as our main team sport for boys. It was also a priority to establish sound discipline throughout the school. In this I had the full support of the staff, so we were in a position to reassure parents that the school was taking a traditional approach to discipline. We also reviewed the curriculum to blend the old with the new and we developed a range of activities designed to enhance the pupils' school experience. For example, we were one of the first secondary schools to embark on a supported programme of after-school study periods, thanks to funding from the Prince's Trust and matched funding from our devolved budget.

SIGNIFICANT CHANGES

Being one of the first schools to have its budget devolved by the local authority facilitated many of the initiatives and ideas in my early stages as head teacher. This allowed me to scrap hundreds of ancient tables and chairs, purchase new computers and make alterations to the building and classrooms. Staff, parents and pupils genuinely believed I had discovered the secrets of alchemy. The benefits of this financial management to the morale of everyone were clear from the early days.

Soon after my arrival, major reviews of management tasks and responsibilities were undertaken. This aspect had not previously benefited from close attention. For the first time in the life of the school there was a focus on the management aspects of the curriculum, personnel and the budget. In this I enjoyed the support of my four senior colleagues, only two of whom remained from the previous administration. All of them fully supported the move towards a much tighter management structure. The curriculum contained many anomalies and did not conform fully to national guidelines. There were historical imbalances in the staffing which left some subject areas under-represented and there was no system for allocating budgets to those responsible for curriculum subjects.

Policies were quickly addressed, with the support of staff volunteers on different committees. A two-year phased implementation of new structures led to a more appropriate curriculum for the pupils. A new strategy was introduced to make subject leaders more accountable through annual reviews, departmental visits, scrutiny of examination results and an open-door approach to all staff who wished to discuss matters with the head. My door has remained open ever since! In the first few years a number of key policies were developed. In addition, management issues such as development planning, delegated resource management, performance indicators, and curricular innovation including the 5–14 programme, Standard Grade revision and the early stages of the Higher Still programme were all addressed.

Other policies were less overt, such as our strategic approach to public relations. All possible avenues were used to instil public confidence in the school and to raise our profile in the town. A monthly newsletter for parents was started and we ensured that there were regular school reports in the local newspaper. We extended existing good connections with the world of business and industry and introduced new design features to the school handbook and public documentation. The latter exercises were enhanced by the introduction of a school logo, following a competition amongst the pupils. The 'thinker' logo is now used on most of our publications along with the original school crest, which included the motto *Virtute ac labore*, 'virtue through hard work'.

The systems and structures of the school were reorganized. The pastoral guidance team was realigned on a vertical system with clear responsibilities for specific registration groups. Senior teacher remits were revised and focused their contribution on the management of the school. Staff, pupils and parents became clearly aware of each person's role in the organization of the school and procedures were put in place to ensure that the system could be explained directly to pupils. For instance, frequent assemblies were introduced for each year group, and a pupil council was set up to give each class an elected representative, meeting regularly with a senior member of staff. These mechanisms formed strands of an informal communications policy that has to be at the heart of successful school management. 'If they don't know what you're doing, they won't know why you're doing it, so they won't like it and it won't work!'

MAIN PROBLEMS AND SOLUTIONS

With a fairly small staff turnover, one major problem was how to carry the very experienced, and sometimes quite disillusioned, middle managers with me and my senior colleagues. I already knew many of them from my previous time at Cumbernauld High, over 10 years earlier, so it was not difficult to adopt an informal approach with them, encouraging first-name terms and using as much of my sense of humour as was legally possible. This practice easily transferred to the majority of staff, but there remain to this day a few who continue to address me as 'Mr Doig', and one or two who refer to me in much less complimentary terms. However, there is now a clear recognition throughout the staff that they are valued and appreciated and this was formally recognized through our attainment of the IIP standard. The school, its structures and its staff have been measured externally against nationally agreed criteria and our success entitles us to display the IIP logo. This in turn proclaims our status to all visitors to the school.

A second big issue was the attitude of many pupils to their work. Often they seemed to place little value on their achievements and did not have a particularly high level of self-esteem. This partly derived, as I soon discovered, from their perception of not being valued in school. Recognition of achievement was started, culminating in two annual award ceremonies. It was very much a 'right first time' initiative and was warmly welcomed by staff, parents and pupils alike. Merit certificates are awarded for academic excellence and commendations for outstanding work throughout the school year. From the beginning, the ceremonies were well attended but each year the audience has grown to the extent that all those who wish to be present can barely be accommodated in the school hall. The agenda has now moved on to the raising achievement policy of North Lanarkshire Council.

There are many possibilities for youngsters to be given recognition for their achievements, whether in the classroom or outside. For example, each year about 20 per cent of 15-year-olds spend a week at the Outward Bound centre at Loch Eil, near Fort William. They return with a tangible feeling of achievement. Regardless of the details of such arrangements, there is a real need for school leaders to establish a variety of opportunities to allow young people to gain self-confidence, learn new skills and interact with others of their own age. If we are to tap into the potential of future citizens, their education cannot be confined to the classroom but must also be delivered in the wider world.

Not all initiatives have been wholly successful. We introduced a range of school uniform items: sweatshirts, polo shirts and T-shirts. They carried the school logo and in the school colours of black, white and grey. These proved to be very popular amongst parents and younger pupils, indeed our most recent order was worth over £4000, but did not strike the right chord with older pupils who resolutely do not wear the approved items. We have traditional school ties but these are not widely worn and, although many pupils adhere to our dress code, we do not have the power to insist on a school uniform. Interestingly, all the schools in Cumbernauld have tried and have only partially succeeded in introducing school uniforms.

Despite our best efforts to raise pupil attainment, this has proved to be a slow and frustrating experience. Results have varied over the years, although the school's overall performance has consistently exceeded expectations based on the socio-economic factors outlined earlier. The year 1998–99 was the first time that our results had remained steady, rather than fluctuating from the previous year. The pupils could certainly perform better in national examinations. Other schools in the town tend to have better overall results and we continually find that we have to work harder to maintain our proximity to them. However, we have plans to put a sharper focus on individual pupil results, with a view to ensuring that we can identify underachievement at a sufficiently early stage. We have introduced a new focus to our supported study programme, featuring subject workshops after school in almost all departments. We also have a study adviser scheme, in which senior pupils deemed to be at risk of underachieving are allocated to a teacher, who supports and advises them as they progress through their senior years.

Other initiatives currently under development will further enhance the provision for underachievers. Firstly, in collaboration with the Prince's Trust and the local authority, we have set up the first 'Fifteen Club' in Scotland. It follows the model successfully established in a number of local education authorities in England. A small group of 15 pupils is identified from the underachievers. They receive dedicated support from an advisor, in our case a promoted guidance teacher, for 10 per cent of the school week. A programme of activities has been specially developed to enhance decision-making skills, self-confidence and motivation, requiring a contribution from every member of the club. Rewards can be negotiated and the scheme has attracted support from several large organizations in Cumbernauld, allowing club members to organize an outing to a place of their own choice.

The second initiative involves a bid that has been submitted to the Local Education Authority Excellence Fund to set up a pupil support base within the school. This project will target disaffected pupils for whom the curriculum presents particular problems of motivation and concentration, but who nevertheless have academic potential. If the bid is successful, a teacher will supervise the group of pupils for all or part of the week, working with the learning support department to provide appropriate, differentiated work until pupils are ready to be re-integrated into their normal classes. A major difficulty in these two approaches is that they are heavily dependent on external funding, whether from the Prince's Trust or from the local authority. Every school in Scotland has suffered a reduction in its devolved budget and it has become increasingly difficult for school leaders to sustain developments from within their own resources.

PRESENT STATE OF THE SCHOOL

Cumbernauld High is in good shape. The roll has risen again in 1999–2000, including a rise in the unit, although a rationalization programme in the primary sector means that the school lost its intake from four associated primary schools in August 2000. To some extent this is likely to be offset by growth from the developing areas within our catchment, but eventually we will have to work harder to maintain our current share of the educational market.

We are installing an information and communications technology (ICT) network, part of a £2 million programme across all North Lanarkshire's secondary schools. This has created access to the Internet and a school-wide intranet. One drawback is that many of our existing computers are too old to operate effectively on the new network. Considerable investment is required to bring our hardware up to date in order to support teaching and learning with ICT across the curriculum.

The school is well staffed compared with many similar schools in other local authorities, thanks to our enhancement for the level of deprivation suffered by many of the pupils. Our pupil : teacher ratio is about 13.5 : 1, a figure which compares favourably with many other countries. Less satisfactory is the morale of the staff. In common with all Scottish schools, we are suffering from a long-term malaise within the profession. This is currently being addressed by a government enquiry into teachers' pay and conditions of service.

MANAGEMENT AND LEADERSHIP

Management style

My management style is to lead by example, setting the standard for senior colleagues in terms of professional relationships, attention to detail, forward planning, financial control and curriculum management. I developed a model of shared responsibility and accountability for my senior colleagues and encouraged middle managers to adopt a similar approach in their departments. This has led to the delegation of decision-making to the lowest appropriate level.

With the 'open-door' policy, all staff have access to advice, information and support from the senior management team, but there is a major drawback to this arrangement. There is no scope for uninterrupted work, and members of the senior staff are constantly on call. Time management thus becomes difficult and the pressures arising from the random nature of demands on our time mean that there is little opportunity for quality time. Some years ago I undertook a course on managing time that encouraged me to set aside a fixed period each day when everyone would know that I was not available. This would create time for strategic thinking and planning. The problem with this idea is that, in the words of one New York high school principal, 'the curriculum don't come knocking at your door'. It is very difficult to ignore a plea for help from a pupil or colleague in order to ensure one's own peace of mind.

Participative management

Much of the school's decision-making process is through consultation and discussion. The process usually starts at senior management team meetings and is fed through the subject departments for discussion among the whole teaching staff, resulting in a high degree of ownership throughout the school. All major policies derive from the school development plan supported by a structure of staff committees that tease out the implementation issues. I myself chair the development plan committee, emphasizing the central importance of this process to the overall management of the school. Senior managers chair a number of strategic committees, placing them at the heart of the decision-making process. In the course of my eight years as head, we have developed whole-school policies on a variety of topics from discipline to bullying, differentiation to raising achievement, and support for learning to staff development.

Curriculum management

The development plan operates on a three-year cycle and each subject department is required to articulate its contribution to the overall plan. Targets and priorities are agreed at the start of the cycle following discussion within the committee and consultation among the staff of the school, a process soon to be extended to include pupils and parents. However, there are considerable drawbacks to the development planning process. Some of the priorities are determined by government initiatives and some by local authority policies. Since both of these bodies are political, the external priorities are open to change without warning if the agenda changes after local or national elections. In Scotland we have argued for a long time for a commitment from central government to a development plan at national level, in order to avoid the constant demands on schools to incorporate new initiatives in their development plans. For some strange reason this has yet to happen!

Some years ago, Her Majesty's Inspectorate issued a document to all Scottish schools outlining the key areas covered when inspecting a school. It detailed a total of 33 performance indicators (PI) that further described these general areas. A key task for school leaders is to relate development planning to PIs and to ensure that, over the three years of a planning cycle, all or most of the indicators are covered. This makes planning an artificial process since many of the issues important to an individual school are not included in the PIs. However, if we try to incorporate additional priorities into the plan, we run the risk of overloading the system and achieving few targets. School leaders are therefore not free to plan the priorities of their own school as they must take full account of national and local authority demands. The management process at times becomes subservient to the current political agenda.

Communications

Communications are of paramount importance in a delegated management structure. Regular meetings of the senior management team and of subject departments are essential to the smooth running of the school. Each senior manager has the responsibility for links with certain subjects as well as a remit that covers a range of whole-school management issues.

Curriculum monitoring

Monitoring of the curriculum, teaching and learning is achieved through these departmental links, both informally and formally. Informal monitoring is possible by virtue of a regular presence by senior managers in every department. This link manager is also available to give advice and support when required. The more formal monitoring mechanisms include an annual review process, requiring the preparation of a written report by subject leaders. This forms the agenda for a discussion between the subject leader, the head teacher and the link manager. The discussion usually takes place during the first term of the school year and includes an analysis of recent examination results, a review of the department's contribution to the school development plan and an overview of staff development activities.

Another formal exercise is the programme of classroom visits undertaken by the head teacher and the depute head, usually in the second term. These are intimated a day or two in advance and include visits to as many different classes as possible in each subject area. The focus is on observation of teaching and learning and the visits are followed by attendance of the head or depute at a department meeting, when issues arising from the visit can be discussed. The existence of these established formal procedures does not diminish the importance of the head's continuous presence about the school, not only at intervals and lunch times but during class time as well. If possible, I will visit a class to see an individual member of staff or a pupil rather than telephoning or sending for them. This can disturb a lesson but there is no denying the impact that is derived from the head teacher coming into the classroom, whether it brings good news or bad!

Quality assurance

Each year, examination results are scrutinized and compared against the results from previous years, from neighbouring schools, from across the local authority and against national figures. Within the school, the performance of departments can be compared using a standard statistical package. From these statistics we are able to gauge the extent to which subjects have added value to pupils' results. We can identify subjects where results are significantly above others, and praise them. Those that seem to be underperforming are supported.

A recent innovation has been the introduction of a school-based standards and quality report. This is based on a self-evaluation of the school's progress against selected PIs in each of the seven main categories, plus a review of the elements of the Local Education Authority's raising achievement strategy on which we have focused. This report takes its format from the generic subject reports now being published by HMI, based on their inspections of Scottish schools. The documents will contribute to the local authority's own standards and quality report, which is made available to the local councillors and eventually to HMI as they introduce inspections of each Scottish local authority.

Taken together, these approaches offer a high degree of accountability for individual schools and are an integral part of a delegated school management model now commonplace across Scotland. Head teachers have control over their school's budgeted costs, including staffing. Although we are subject to rigorous checks on our expenditure, we have a considerable amount of flexibility to control spending at school level. For this task the school has an administrative and finance assistant whose job is to manage and track the £3 million devolved budget for the school, plus four primary schools, two special schools and a nursery unit.

CONCLUSION

Effective leadership derives from both management experience and skills, and I am fortunate to have spent almost 20 years in senior posts. During this time I have had access to training in a wide variety of management issues. I have enjoyed excellent support from my senior colleagues and from the staff throughout the school, teaching and non-teaching. Along the way I have made some mistakes and had a few disappointments, but overall I have enjoyed the challenges of school management and I look forward to those that are still to come.

'All good experience!'

RICHARD FAWCETT

I was appointed as a newly qualified geographer in September 1968 at Theale Grammar School, Berkshire, by Ken Shield, the founding head teacher. A strong community school, it became comprehensive in 1973 and was renamed Theale Green School. Ken exuded enthusiasm and was keen to see staff take responsibility. Promotion followed to head of house after two years at Theale. The house structure was very strong. Each had its own Parent Teacher Association (PTA) and heads of house were, along with the senior staff, the policy formers. It was an ideal place to start a career. 'All good experience!' was Ken Shield's phrase, so often heard when confiding in him that an event was tricky to handle, or when one had bitten off just that bit too much.

Deputy headship at Dorcan School, Swindon, followed. This expanding, purpose-built comprehensive school grew to 1600 students. An amalgam of roles included responsibility for discipline, the administration of subject choices and leading curriculum development. Dorcan was a challenging new-town situation with demanding, yet responsive students. The school was innovative and forward-looking.

I became deputy principal of Frome College, Somerset, in 1980. The college was unique in combining secondary and further education provision under one leadership. My brief was to bring its two sectors together. It was an amazing assignment. The myths about further education were alive and well in the 1300-strong school, as were those of the school sector in the tiny further education unit grafted on during local government reorganization. The creation of the county of Avon had left Frome's further education annexe in Somerset, cut off from the main college in Radstock.

The time in Frome coincided with the expansion of the remit of the Manpower Services Commission. In a memorable afternoon's meeting the principal, John Fisher, was successful in obtaining funding for five new full-time courses along with the necessary accommodation, equipment and staffing. John was an entrepreneur and breaker of the mould. In 1986 I was promoted to head teacher at Thurston Upper School, Suffolk. The school was renamed Thurston Community College in 1999 to more closely reflect its role.

THURSTON COMMUNITY COLLEGE

SOCIO-ECONOMIC CONTEXT

Thurston Community College serves 500 square kilometres of Suffolk countryside to the east of Bury St Edmunds. It is a 13–18 co-educational comprehensive school with 1300 students, nearly 400 being in the sixth form. Students come from over 40 villages, up to 20 kilometres away. Some have never visited local centres such as Norwich and Cambridge. Many families have lived in the same village for generations. Others are very mobile, having recently moved into the area. Commuting to Cambridge and London is common.

The catchment area is complex with a wide social mix. Both affluence and pockets of rural deprivation and isolation exist. Some students live in locations where another house cannot be seen. Many more are from villages in which facilities are at most one shop, a pub and a church. The bus shelter may be the students' only legal public meeting place. The college also serves three large villages, all recently expanded, each with over 3000 inhabitants. When compared with other schools in Suffolk, the school is in the top eight in terms of ability of entrant. Fewer than 5 per cent are eligible for free school meals.

THE SCHOOL IN 1986

Thurston Upper School opened in 1973 as a purpose-built school on a greenfield site. Opening coincided with comprehensive reorganization. The previous head teacher had been in post a number of years, more recently on secondment.

Many of the staff, particularly at middle management level, had been at the school since 1973.

In 1986, there did not appear to be any clear vision, possibly an outcome of the interregnum. It was really a 13–16 comprehensive school. In the sixth form, students were selected for A-level using an absolute criterion of five high grades at O-level. In the main school, academic banding created divisions. There was a top group and a remedial group of students, taught by a 'separate' remedial staff. The curriculum had not developed for some time.

Staff were minimally involved in decision-making and planning. The head teacher had met with deputies, but there were no task or cross-curricular groups and no accountability structure. Everyone in middle management and senior posts reported to the head teacher. Department teams were strong and both staff and students identified positively with the house pastoral system.

The PTA was selective, in that parents paid a subscription to join. There was no business or community contact of any substance, no contact with further education colleges and the media were held at arm's length. There was a feeling of isolation.

INTERNAL AND EXTERNAL PRESSURES ON THE SCHOOL

Some staff, including many heads of department, wished to let things be. Early moves to broaden the sixth form, particularly a proposed vocational course, were met with reluctance by some, including the head of sixth. Others were desperate for a move. The head of remedial was one such colleague. He described how his students, the separate remedial stream, rushed into classrooms and slammed the doors shut to taunts of 'Rem!' shouted down corridors.

Externally, there was virtually no pressure to change. Suffolk Local Education Authority (LEA) had no agenda for change particular to the school. Parents were apparently satisfied and the community thought the school was good. Creating the agenda for school development had to come from within, led by the head teacher.

THE AGENDA FOR CHANGE

Evolution rather than revolution has characterized the changes made at Thurston, centered on opportunities for student success. A review at the start of headship led to many staff working groups looking at diverse areas of the school. All staff were encouraged to join, whatever their status. What had been static started to change.

Curriculum change has been a strong, continuing thread. The pre-16 curriculum was initially restructured to remove streaming. Technology, co-ordinated (double) science and a modern foreign language became part of a reshaped core. Optional subjects were added, such as humanities, drama and creative textiles. The General National Vocational Qualification (GNVQ) Part One was established in manufacturing and business studies, both as part of a national pilot. Later, art and design, and leisure and tourism, were added. Early involvement in national reforms allowed us, in some small measure, to shape their development. The learning development department grew out of the remedial section, with a brief for all students needing support. Post-16, the Technical and Vocational Education Initiative (TVEI) led to a Certificate of Pre-Vocational Education (CPVE) course and, more recently, GNVQ courses at intermediate and advanced level have created comprehensive provision for 16- to 18-year-olds.

In 1986, there were few written policies or departmental schemes of work. Today, the required policies are in place. Keeping abreast of needs and updating policies requires a formal review structure. I believe the key to successful policy formulation lies in real staff involvement. The usual model at Thurston has been for a senior member of staff to take the lead in whole-school policy formulation, working with a team of volunteers or an appropriate group of staff. However, ensuring that policies are followed long term is much more difficult than creating them. The culture does not always promote consensus, which is easier to write about than to achieve. Individuality and professional freedom are still quoted as valid reasons for variation!

In the first year of headship I created a senior team and shadow staffing structure. The responsibility points attached to posts were declared for the first time. There are now clear lines of accountability. Each of the three deputy heads has responsibility for the work of a group of middle managers. The benefit of this relationship between the college's leadership team and team leaders cannot be overemphasized.

The governors were brought into greater contact with the realities of school life, good and bad. A head teacher must make a decision about his openness with governors and the depth of their involvement in school life. My warts-and-all approach brought with it a continuing debate about the boundaries between the roles of governor and head teacher.

The college is growing. It will soon have 1600 students. The three houses have become six. The wish for each head of house to work with a small team of seven tutors has, so far, been successful. Main school tutor groups include Year 9, 10 and 11 students (ages 13–16). There is no inter-year rivalry and a strong house identity remains.

The growth of the support staff, in number and breadth of role, is significant. In common with many schools, current expenditure on support staff outstrips resources nominally allocated. Overall, the strategy has been to focus the work of teachers on learning and teaching. Some of the resources once designated to management salaries now pay for secretarial and support staff. The bursar has become business manager with a wide-ranging role, a delegated budget and responsibility for buildings and catering. Heads of house have secretarial support, initially financed from a diminution in their non-contact time. A member of the office staff, nominally led by a member of the senior team, completes staff absence cover. Low levels of funding and higher than average individual staff costs have inhibited ambition. For example, there is still no information and communications technology (ICT) network manager, nor premises manager.

There must be a central thrust in school leadership. Beliefs must be openly and clearly stated and the head must be willing to articulate these. The school ethos or central vision must be allowed to develop within the staff. There is no future in transporting a vision into a school and telling people to hold it. They will not believe in it even if, on the surface, they go along with the vision. After some years, 'a community committed to success, raising standards through high expectations', emerged as the vision for the school. It reflected my personal set of beliefs, staff views and the benefits that would accrue to the students.

THE PROBLEMS: RIDING THE TIDE

Headship has been for me a continuous learning opportunity, in college, with the Secondary Heads Association (SHA) and in pursuing my own professional development. The problems, both the day to day and the once in a lifetime, need to be seen as opportunities to learn. The day everything appears done is the day the big problem arises! Complacency is the root of certain disaster.

Thurston is not the place where difficulties are stark and obvious. The college is not in a socially deprived area, students are largely amenable, staff are well qualified, there is a sense of order and student achievement has increased year on year. So, where is the challenge? It is in confronting what is wrong, but much more in the largely unacknowledged area of continuous work trying to make the satisfactory good and the good very good. It is not allowing the informal to become casual. It is confronting performance that may seem fine, but against national comparitors is not. It is also about making the most of being a community resource. At the other extreme, it is in dealing with specific crises.

Learning: the central focus of the college

League tables are long on figures and short on perspective. Successful learning is wider than statistical achievement. Learning rose prominently to the top of the agenda during participation in the Improving the Quality of Education for All (IQEA) project undertaken with Suffolk LEA and the University of Cambridge in 1992. Some felt a tick could be put against learning when the Office for Standards in Education (Ofsted) report on Thurston in 1997 declared that all teaching was satisfactory or better and had only one key issue for action, 'ensure that all students receive their proper curriculum entitlement in religious education' in the sixth form.

However, following discussion, we chose three developmental themes as a focus for future learning development: the application of student performance data, ICT and an emphasis on supporting individual students. A senior member of staff now has a strong grasp on student data and its interpretation. The college has become data-rich. Student performance data includes the information from a variety of sources: Ofsted, feeder middle schools, key-stage data, national examinations and value-added measures. The LEA provides detailed comparisons of student progress in all Suffolk schools with students of a similar ability and across the county as a whole. Separate boy and girl performance data is available. Recently, there has been a change in staff attitude to student performance data. Confrontation of issues has become collegiate, along with a willingness to share in solutions, especially where the data is related to a particular teaching group.

A focus on the use of ICT in learning has also moved the college forward. Bidding (unsuccessfully) for technology college status focused the staff to think about ICT and learning. A learning centre was created for integrated learning systems and the expansion of Internet access. Enabling teachers to be part of the ICT vision was vital. It led to an early start in whole-staff ICT training and the acquisition of staff computers using government financial support. The benefits to class-based learning are being seen in student motivation and progress, though the shoots are still green and tender at times. A bonus materialized from liaison with local schools. At a committee meeting to discuss a social event involving the college and contributory schools, casual conversation with a parent turned into £50,000 of tangible support, software and hardware for creating an intranet and further Web-based learning developments.

The third plank in the learning focus has been the use as mentors of adults from many occupations and students. Sixth-form students are expected to make a college community commitment. This has increased the number volunteering as mentors. Each has been trained to work alongside younger students, often in class, in a wide range of activities from reading and writing to coursework support and basic friendship. Thurston has its share of underachievers and disrupted family lives. For some students the mentor is the only person with whom they have real conversation in depth on a regular basis.

At the heart of the community

There have been significant community developments for Thurston. Indeed, the college has gained the Schools Curriculum Award three times for its involvement 'at the heart of the community'. First, my early decision to embrace the media, now common amongst schools, was less usual at the time. It was not welcomed by a significant number of staff with long memories, as the local press had critically reported a Thurston student protest some years earlier. Eyebrows were raised higher when, after an isolated incident involving possession of cannabis on the site, I was asked for and gave an interview on site to regional television.

The culture of any school is deeply influenced by past events. Some staff think it is not for the head teacher to own up to failure, mistakes or regret. However, I have come to believe that, along with celebrating success and presenting the college in the best light, it is important to acknowledge when things are not as they should be. 'Tell parents first, before the media informs them and the public,' has been a useful maxim.

Putting resources into the college prospectus, separate sixth-form brochure and the other printed material sent home, has paid dividends. This is not solely a matter of full-colour production. Of greater significance is the valuing of students, highlighting achievement and including student views about the college. The recent introduction of a regular fortnightly newsletter, removing most other mass written communication, has been welcomed but the school needs to make more effort to develop the full worth of this publication.

Bringing the community into the college has been a long haul. There was hardly any activity outside school hours in 1986. My belief is that this is a central school role and has meant careful planning, risk-taking and hours of work by governors, staff and parents. For example, facilities have to be marketed with a view to attracting people to college rather than profit making. We now have a floodlit multi-games area that is used intensively. A pass scheme for casual use of the college fields has been introduced. The PTA, now supporting all parents without subscription, is active in its own niche market. Running events such as fashion shows and quiz nights which involve students, parents and staff, provides a focus. A seniors' luncheon club is supported, with food cooked by the school kitchen and served by students. The National Youth Orchestra, Kenny Ball, Eliza Carthy, Herman's Hermits and The Searchers are some who have performed in

Thurston's 350-seat auditorium, bringing risks, profits and occasional losses. An extensive set of evening classes is now run on site by the local further education college. Even though there is no other organization or finance to support such involvement, I firmly believe that the returns enhance the learning community.

The community is also active internationally. From opportunities to teach English to Danish students to annual expeditions including Namibia, Bolivia, Mexico and Mozambique, encouraging students to leave the comforts of Suffolk is important.

There have been failures. Some initiatives have been too person-specific. For example, a creeping and subtle loss of contact with industrialists and other employers has occurred. In spite of a community board meeting termly to review the college involvement with the community and a growth in mentoring, the formal input by business into the curriculum for 13- to 16-year-olds has withered. Who is responsible? In the absence of a nominated person, I am. It is an example of the eye off the ball. There is still much more to do.

Leading in crisis times

Every school has its crises. Some events are seen as a crisis in one context yet relatively day-to-day matters in others. However, the sudden death of a member of staff on the school premises would be an appallingly sad event anywhere and demand much of the head teacher.

So it was when one of the most loved teachers, the head of science, collapsed in school one evening. He was Rick. He died two days later, never regaining consciousness. Such an event is a tragedy above all for the family. But it is also devastating for a school. We lost a man who was an inspirational teacher and the writer and performer of folk songs. He always made everyone laugh and went out of his way for everyone, especially the students who found life tough.

What can you do in such a situation? I gave it all my time. Running the school became the responsibility of others. As far as possible, I dealt personally with everyone involved in the crisis. The family, the staff and the students all had needs. I also worked closely with the people who could help see us through subsequent days and weeks. In Rick's case, it was some of the senior team, two of the staff closest to him and the chair of governors whose wisdom and calm were invaluable.

Telling Rick's wife what had happened, talking with the family, informing Rick's tutor group and then the school, all occupied my time. Making sure that comfort and counselling were provided, dealing with the inevitable media enquiries, arranging for the school event to commemorate Rick's life, all these were important matters and made strong personal demands.

Help comes from unexpected quarters. Those were the days of local authority control overstaffing, including strict guidelines about supply cover. There was no help to enable many staff to go the church service. However, head teachers and senior staff from all over the area volunteered to stand in. We joked, we needed to, over tea with them after our return from church, about this being the only time six head teachers would be teaching in the school at one time.

I found it invaluable to think with others, trying to keep ahead of events. A charity in Rick's name was started and many events have been organized to raise money. One close staff friend has been sponsored to cycle the length of the United Kingdom, and across both the United States and Australia. The interest on investments now enables college students, for whom involvement would otherwise be impossible, to participate in ventures to extend their horizons. Rick would have been pleased.

THURSTON COMMUNITY COLLEGE TODAY

The college is about to take steps forward in developing its role as a learning community. New buildings for post-16 education are in the pipeline. They will hopefully make tangible the view that a community learning centre and library, and possibly a doctors' surgery or health centre all on the one site, will benefit people of all ages, both in the college and community.

Structurally, a focus on what supports an effective learning community for the future is being explored. New staff roles are being discussed and a revised staffing model is being created. The vision for the future of the school aims to encompass many of the views expressed in the journal *Headlines* (SHA, 2000).

LEADERSHIP

Having been the leader of the college for 14 years, there is no escaping the fact that I am responsible for current practice and provision! The context and demands of the college have changed and with them the leadership styles and approaches.

What has influenced my leadership styles? Undoubtedly, head teachers with whom I have worked have been particularly significant. The enthusiasm of Ken Shield and the entrepreneurialism of John Fisher have been exemplars. Membership and active involvement in the SHA has been an invaluable opportunity to learn and to give to the wider educational picture. To be elected by colleagues as the SHA president for 2000–01 was the greatest honour professionally. Recent completion of an educationally-focused international Master's degree in business administration (MBA) has been formative and eye-opening. Experience teaches a great deal, as does significant professional development. One is left to ponder the effect of one's own leadership on others.

Leadership models provide a perspective on which to reflect. The Industrial Society developed its action-centred leadership model around the three areas of achieving tasks, building teams and developing individuals. Whilst some would claim it to be old fashioned, even out of date, there is much to commend in its simplicity. I have found that thinking about the relationship between tasks, teams and individuals is no bad starting place when reflecting on my own leadership.

Leadership today demands vision, creativity, sensitivity and subsidiarity (West-Burnham, 1997: 116). The subsidiarity principle is outlined by Handy (1989: 100) '... it is an injustice ... for a larger and higher organization to arrogate to itself functions which can be performed efficiently by smaller and lower bodies'.

Giving teams and individuals responsibility, authority, resource control and decision-making powers without reference is what subsidiarity is all about. I have a long way to go in fulfilling this! The 'without reference' aspect is the significant difficulty for me, but I am sure it is right.

Leadership is very different from management. The head teacher will be engaged in both. West-Burnham (1997: 117) sums up the difference succinctly:

Leading is concerned with:	*Managing is concerned with:*
vision	implementations
strategic issues	operational issues
transformation	transaction
ends	means
people	systems
doing the right things	doing things right

I am convinced that head teachers must be concerned with all of these leadership areas. If not, then it is likely that they will remain absolutely or relatively ignored, or taken up by others.

How the head teacher approaches leadership is a matter of personal style and conscious or intuitive choice, most likely a mixture of the two. Goleman (2000) has provided a useful up-to-date overarching leadership model that I have found valuable in reflecting about my work. His starting point is that getting results is the essence of leadership. Reporting research by Hay McBer, he defines six leadership styles:

- coercive (demanding immediate compliance);
- authoritative (having a clear vision of where you want to get to, but giving freedom as to how to get there);
- affiliative (creating emotional bonds and harmony);
- democratic (building consensus through participation);
- pacesetting (expecting excellence and self-direction); and
- coaching (developing people for the future).

Each is based on different components of emotional intelligence, the ability to manage our relationships and ourselves effectively. In essence, emotional intelligence is made up of four capabilities:

- self-awareness;
- self-management;
- social awareness;
- social skill.

On emotional intelligence, Goleman (2000: 80) explores the sets of competencies of which each capability is composed:

Self-awareness	*Self-management*	*Social awareness*	*Social skills*
• emotional self-awareness	• trustworthiness	• empathy	• visionary leadership
• accurate self-assessment	• conscientiousness	• organization	• influence
• self-confidence	• adaptability	• service orientation	• developing others
	• achievement orientation		• communication
	• initiative		• change catalyst
	• self-control		• conflict management
			• building bonds
			• teamwork and collaboration

As head teachers know, relying solely on one style of leadership to obtain results does not work. Different events require different styles, for example, the contrast between a response to a furious parent and long-term development of learning. The effect that the head teacher's style has on the school's working environment, the climate, cannot be underestimated. Research, including that of Hay McBer, has shown there are six factors that influence working environment:

- how free people feel to innovate;
- people's sense of responsibility to the school;
- the level of standards people set;
- people's sense of accuracy about performance feedback and rewards;
- clarity as to what the school is trying to accomplish and the values it holds;
- the level of commitment to the purpose of the school.

The leadership style of the head teacher will affect each aspect of the working environment. The research showed, for example, that authoritative, affiliative, democratic and coaching styles have a positive effect on climate.

At Thurston, the styles I have used have not only varied with the people and the matter in hand, but also taken into account the culture of the staff as a whole. I have rarely used a coercive style with staff. An example would be in reminding someone of an instruction when clearly it has been flouted. I have, however, used it in setting out the parameters of behaviour and action with students. Sometimes that is necessary. In general I believe that coercion damages innovation and commitment. Where top-down leadership exists in abundance, staff quickly give up having ideas and taking responsibility.

Enthusiasm and vision are at the root of the authoritative style. It is best used where a clear statement is needed about where a school is going, where a change of policy is requested, or where there is a need for the staff to work rapidly together. This approach has worked well, for example in preparing for an Ofsted inspection and for setting out initially why the college should be involved in initial teacher training, when it was a contentious issue with staff.

The affiliative style, where people come forward for help in difficult circumstances, is vital in times of great stress. It was invaluable in pulling the staff back together after an incident where a few students had behaved particularly badly, a very rare occurrence at Thurston. That was a time when my loyalty to staff was critical, where people needed to be valued for their willingness to show emotion about what had happened and have their feelings recognized as important. Looking back, cold analysis sounds calculating. It is somewhat. You need to know what approach to take in difficult circumstances, but you must also be able to employ it genuinely rather than implementing a textbook solution.

In the long haul of raising standards of learning, much more complex than solely improving exam results, I have often used a democratic style to explore ways forward. When you need other people's ideas and their commitment and are yourself uncertain as to the detail of where you wish to be or the direction to take, then it is invaluable. Used well, it is disarming. Convincing staff that there is no master plan waiting to be wheeled out, whatever their ideas may be, has been sometimes difficult to achieve.

In the pacesetting style the leader personally sets very high performance standards. Everyone is expected to do things better and faster all the time. If expectations are not spelled out and feedback is not given, the approach is destructive, but there is a place for such a style. Where a team is very skilled and capable, it works well for a short time. The senior team at Thurston has had its ups and downs, as do all teams. When working at its best, the team has responded well to pacesetting. For example, clear definition is required when putting in intensive work on budget cutbacks in times of difficulty.

Using the coaching style helps staff identify their personal strengths and aspirations. It focuses on personal development, not on the task in hand. Helping staff to develop by agreeing roles and giving them challenging responsibilities is important. Giving feedback on performance also has a positive impact on the school climate. From talking through the conversation with the difficult parent, to drawing out positively the lessons where something went wrong, constructive concern is important to demonstrate. I have found some staff more receptive than others to this approach! I am sure I should use it more often.

Using a number of styles, and moving from one to another as appropriate, is vital and can become the culture of the leader: 'the way things are done here'. A particular problem may require a battery of different responses. There is certainly no place for the overt checklist approach. It has to become second nature. We can all develop skills further. Intuition rooted in understanding acquired by critical self-analysis, and practice based on theory and learning are powerful.

Some nuggets have come with headship experience. On Industrial Society leadership courses, Sir Peter White used to give a lecture full of valuable sound bites from beginning to end.

> Leaders are paid to sit on volcanoes. Don't expect a salary and a round of applause. No crying on parade. It is lonely at the top, but you can't lead from a crowd. Schools, like fish, go bad from the head downwards. Cultivate the art of living in the here and now.

There is no replacing such wisdom. It is worth framing!

A counter to all models and ideals is the simple fact that people remember most the small things you do for them. You will never please everyone, but the time given to listening to a problem, the public word of thanks, a quick visit to see the cooks, the personal support over an unruly student or a person falsely accused, are all remembered. If making a cup of tea for someone is above the head teacher, then a dimension of leadership is lost!

For me, optimism, laughter and enjoyment are crucial. In the end, like Ken Shield's 'all good experience', I am sure that the way people behave and the results they bring to their work reflect the leader's personal style and willingness to learn and grow.

REFERENCES

Goleman, D (2000) Leadership that Gets Results, *Harvard Business Review*, **78**, 78–90

Handy, C (1989) *The Age of Unreason*, Arrowsmith Books, London

Secondary Heads Association (March 2000) *Headlines: The journal of the Secondary Heads Association*, **32**, New Venture Publications, London

West-Burnham, J (1997) *Managing Quality in Schools*, Pitman Publishing, London

Putting pupils first

MARC SACKUR

My initial training was as a secondary mathematics teacher. My appointments were in France, followed by a time in a French school in Montreal, Canada. That provided experience of a different system of education, but one that included many French first-language speakers. A further appointment followed in Paris as a teacher in classe préparatoire aux grandes écoles (CPGE), preparing students for university. My first headship was in a small school in Metz, Lorraine, before returning to Paris where I led a school known as JJ and subsequently took up my current position at the Lycée Lakanal. My experience has spanned 24 years of mathematics teaching in the age range 12–20, and 12 years of headship.

SOCIO-ECONOMIC CONTEXT OF FRENCH SCHOOLS

An explanation of the French system will help the reader to understand the educational context. Education is compulsory until 16, but most continue studies until the final examination, the baccalauréat, taken at 18 or 19. Secondary education is divided into two cycles, one to age 16 in a collège, and the other for three years, in a lycée. There are three kinds of lycée, namely general, technological and vocational. There is an increasing trend to establish lycées polyvalents that mix two or even three types of teaching. In general and technological education, the first year of a lycée is not specialized. Pupils study more or less the same subjects with two optional additions.

At the end of the year they have to choose one of the three subjects – literature, economics or sciences – or one of the many subjects in the technological group. The vocational route is chosen right at the end of the collège and is already specialized. There are bridges between vocational and general education according to the results and the ability of the pupil. The curriculum and the amount of time each subject has to be taught are both fixed by the ministry and cannot be changed. The final baccalauréat is also organized at the state level with no local adjustment.

Another important feature of the French system is that in a lycée you can find university teaching taught by selected secondary teachers. In technological schools the diploma of higher technician, brevet de technicien supérieur (BTS), can be found and in general lycées the CPGE, equivalent to the first two years of university, is taught. This leads to the graduate cycle of a university course, by agreement between the lycée and some universities, or, after a competitive examination, to special higher institutes called grandes écoles that specialize in the field of engineering and business.

JJ SCHOOL AND LYCÉE LAKANAL

JJ SCHOOL

The JJ school was a lycée polyvalent with a small amount of general scientific subjects. It was mainly industrial with mechanics, electronics and even a sheet-metalwork section to which it was very difficult to attract pupils. At that time it had 1250 pupils. It was located in an industrial suburb north-west of Paris that had been an important centre since the beginning of the last century, but had suffered a decline. The local rate of unemployment was high. Many inhabitants were immigrants and the lycée had pupils from 30 different nationalities. The lycée also had a vocational part and the bridges from vocational to technical education were easy. The lycée was once famous because, in such an industrial area, being educated at JJ guaranteed local employment and social improvement. Following industrial decline, the situation is now different.

LYCÉE LAKANAL

In contrast, the Lycée Lakanal is located in a well-off area in a southern Parisian suburb. It has 2450 pupils, is mixed, is both a collège and a lycée in general education, and has many CPGEs leading to literature, business or engineering university places. It is a school with a long history and beautiful buildings, but they are difficult to use in the pedagogical context of these times. The teachers and pupils are proud of being in the Lycée Lakanal. The parents are demanding and often ask the school to do what they are unable to do at home. It also has a boarding section.

SIGNIFICANT CHANGES

Introducing change is not easy in the French system. Traditionally, education has been centrally controlled and there is little scope for local initiative. However, a good leader looks for opportunities and some appear below.

Newsletter

I have always felt the need for a school newsletter in order to communicate with everybody. The schools that I have led have both been complex structures. Different schools in the same location and teachers in the same school, but different areas, are often unaware of what is occurring elsewhere. A fortnightly newsletter prepared to a standard framework has improved communication. The first page is devoted to the calendar for the following two weeks. Dates of events, meetings, examinations, conferences and pupil departures are always included. A column is included for teachers, which includes such information as career opportunities. Pedagogical information is also included. The newsletter concludes with cultural information, for example about local events that may be of interest to staff.

Teachers may also provide articles for publication, as long as these do not contain political or union opinions. However, staff do not make sufficient use of this opportunity. The newsletter is also given to parents, so discretion is necessary. As a result, some of the information for staff cannot be written in the newsletter. Since the school has a Web site, the calendar is displayed there and updated every two weeks.

Evaluating the impact of the newsletter is not easy. It is designed to be a transverse mean of communication, but some see it as the voice of the management team. Teachers do use it to disseminate information to colleagues. This was particularly true when the Lycée Lakanal had a European project. On the whole, the letter is read and is useful.

Renovation

JJ had been built at the beginning of the 1960s and was in a very bad state when I arrived. After the student demonstrations of November 1989, the region took the decision to renovate the lycée. An architect began to make plans and discussed these with the head teacher and teachers. He was particularly interested in their view about how to improve the aspect and functioning of the lycée. The plans were precise about the technical workshops, but less so about other areas. My predecessor retired before the work started and when I arrived I had to launch the renovation and implement the work.

Discussions took place with different sections of staff, the architect, the builders and the financing body, the region Ile-de-France. We had to reflect about what was required, since every pedagogical choice has a counterpart in architecture and vice versa. At the same time teaching was maintained. This required numerous timetables to accommodate the phases of the construction. Regular consultation with teachers helped to build their own image of the school.

School projects

Since July 1989 every school in France has been required to have a project that has legal status in the school and must be approved by the board. The idea of this obligation is for every school to have a degree of autonomy. The objective of the school project is to organize this autonomy. It is meant to give a framework in which the resources of the school can be harnessed. This is an important tool for the leadership of the school for two reasons. Firstly, it prevents concealed practices. Future intentions are made clear and everybody knows the direction the school intends to take. The second reason is that it gives individual teachers and teams with new ideas the opportunity to put them into practice. Quite often it allows people to meet and to discuss such projects. Teachers are very individualistic. In both schools that I have led there were no such projects. Only documents that could have been used to contribute to a plan were available. Some examples of projects follow.

- In the Lycée Lakanal some mathematics teachers wanted to have a classroom network linked to the Internet in order to motivate weaker pupils. Some of these were repeating the year. The project was discussed with the board and included in the school project. Then other teachers used the idea to reflect on how they might use such resources in their own classrooms to approve their teaching.

- At the same school we noticed that pupils in their first year had difficulties in coping with all that was new to them: subjects, teachers and the organization of the timetable. A team of teachers, under the supervision of a deputy head, compiled a two-day induction programme to welcome pupils and to explain the difference between a 'collège' and a 'lycée'. It proved to be successful and has since run every year with minor modifications.
- In JJ the idea was to make the lycée more attractive and to raise the level of studies. It had been showed that the level of unemployment decreased as the grade of the diploma rose. We decided to co-operate with a university to build a diploma for young people who already held a BTS.

The means of putting together the school project is sometimes even more important than the project itself. The head teacher must be fully committed. My experimentation with various methods has met with different degrees of success. The first step is to analyse the situation. It is important to collect data in such areas as: the number of pupils; their age; their teachers; examination results; and figures about absenteeism or bullying. A school cannot be summed up in figures, but judgements need to be supported by data. Year-on-year statistics also show how the focus has evolved. What is a project, if it does not change the situation? The last step is the evaluation. What is the real impact of the actions taken? This is the most difficult part, because to answer the question it is necessary to go further than the figures. I have used a number of methods to identify and develop projects.

One was to ask the different communities, teachers, parents and pupils to list three main problems concerning school life. A general meeting was held in order to choose one or two questions, to think about them and make proposals. This method was tried recently but it failed for two reasons. The teachers did not want to make a list and, when they came to the meeting with parents and a small number of pupils, they refused to discuss the parents' needs. On the other hand, parents do sometimes make demands without proposing useful solutions for their own involvement in carrying them out.

Another method is to suspend teaching for half a day and to hold a general meeting during which everything can be discussed. Some major topics appear and committees are created to handle them. The minutes of the meetings are published in the school newsletter. Everybody knows what is going on and joins any committee at any time. At the end of the process another general meeting chooses the main topics, proposals are made and subsequently find their way into the school project.

The topics to be discussed are determined either by the head teacher or by some of the teacher teams. The key criterion is always the needs of the school at that moment. Various people interested in working on the subjects are invited to meet, to exchange proposals and ideas, and at the end to write down their project. This method is often useful when people have ideas about new pedagogical practices or when the general instructions from the ministry raise many difficult questions that need to be addressed.

Repetition of a year

It is a strong tradition in France that a pupil whose work, or sometimes attitude, has not been satisfactory needs to repeat a year in the same form. This is a very difficult situation because it must not be forgotten that in France the curriculum and the subjects are the same for everybody for at least 80 per cent of the time. For example, if a pupil fails on the scientific course he will need to repeat all subjects including those in which he has been successful. This leads to dissatisfaction and demotivation. Of those who repeat their first year at a lycée, 8.5 per cent go on to gain good results, 25.7 per cent are satisfactory and the rest, nearly two-thirds, fail the year again. This has a cost implication, since more forms are needed and therefore more teachers at each level. I have always been convinced that we should not resign ourselves to that situation and have taken action to reduce the number of repeats. The class council can make a proposal at the end of the year and, if the pupil or family does not agree with it, the head teacher has to decide after meeting both parties. A head teacher does have real power to reduce the numbers who have to repeat a year. In the Lycée Lakanal the evolution of the school rate has been a drop from 15 per cent in 1997 to 8 and 10 per cent in the following two years.

At the same time I had to propose to the teachers a pedagogical policy that was designed to help such students with their difficulties. For younger pupils special help is given in small groups. For older students I feel a greater responsibility because the decision to waive the repetition was mine. With the help of some mathematics teachers a project using computers and the Internet was designed. The Internet is used to exchange questions with other schools. Pupils pose questions to those in the second school and they answer them.

LEADERSHIP AND APPROACH

Team spirit

In France, when the head teacher arrives at the school the staff are already there. This is the most challenging part of the job. The school has no autonomy over the appointment of staff. All the appointments are decided at the national level. The criteria are the wishes of the person and a scale that takes into consideration the length of service, family needs and professional value. The head teacher knows that there will be no changes in the staff that can be initiated, except very difficult cases of misbehaviour, which are rare. I have not met any during my career.

The first task that the new head teacher faces is to build a team spirit with the deputy head and the councillor for education (CPE). It is the CPE's responsibility to manage pupil discipline in the school. It is my view that the head must trust those who are already in the school. They know many things that he or she does not know. The head teacher must neither be 'the person who knows best' nor come to the school with ready-made ideas as if there was only one style of leadership that could apply to every school. Having many deputies, in my case three, one each for finance, equipment management and staffing, and five CPEs, I have to delegate and to know the responsibilities of each of them. There are always conflicts at the boundaries. Some want to extend their territory and some want to do as little as possible. Ultimately the head teacher has to take the responsibility for drawing the boundaries.

Regular reporting must be organized so that the head knows what is being done. I must not speak of *my* deputy. Deputy and head teachers belong to the same category of civil servant. One is the head of the school and the other is the deputy head. This simply gives them different responsibilities. The difference between being *my* deputy or the deputy head teacher of the school is important and gives an interesting insight into the kind of relationship that we must have in a French school.

Consensus

One should not expect to run a school in a perpetual consensus. There will always be inevitable conflicts. These are due to the divergent interests of the stakeholders or even different interpretations of what is best for the school or pupils. It is better to have a way of managing conflicts than to try to avoid them at all costs. The first priority must be adult management. People should not act in an emotional way. Although we are not there to love each other, we have a job in common that is to bring our pupils to the highest point that they can reach. When a difficult decision is to be taken that can affect the professional life of members of the community or school it is important to be clear about the stakes. Tricks are inappropriate for they will be discovered one day and subsequently ruin future confidence.

When meeting people and discussing with adults it is very useful, if possible, to bring quantitative evidence that is related to the problem. Everyone should be given the opportunity to present their own reasons and should be listened to, but it is clear that the decision will be the head teacher's. Even if it is impossible to convince everybody that the decision is right, all need to be convinced that it does not spring from a whim, but has been considered carefully. When I left my first headship, a member of staff paid me a compliment by saying, 'we lost time in the beginning, because we thought that there was a trick, and when we noticed there was no trick, it was too late and now you are leaving'.

One of the most difficult tasks of headship is to deal with teachers who, for whatever reasons, have been unsatisfactory in their teaching or have behaved in an unacceptable manner. Often parents inform me, sometimes older pupils and on other occasions I hear by rumour. I must not believe right away what I am told. I always ask for a written report or at least for a formal meeting in my office. Then I meet the teacher and try to have a clear and free conversation with him or her. Sometimes it can be very difficult. In France the quality of pedagogy is not in the hands of the head teacher, but of the pedagogical inspectors. If a question of teacher competence arises, a head teacher asks for a pedagogical inspection and requests the inspector to give advice to the teacher.

If I am convinced that things are within my remit but are not going well, sanctions can be taken. A head teacher can use the mark that has to be given every year to every teacher. Together with the mark given by the pedagogical inspector, the teachers are rated on a scale that determines their salary. The final salary is beyond the authority of the school. Giving a bad mark can therefore slow salary progression. This applies to teachers who are not on the top of the scale. In such a circumstance a head only has the power of his or her own conviction. The teacher may require regular monitoring and professional dialogue in an attempt to foster improvement.

Community

Making the school a real community, and not a juxtaposition of communities, is the head teacher's task. All members have a role to play in the well-being of the school. Before taking an action each should consider the consequences for other members of the community. In JJ many teachers of general subjects (French, English and mathematics) and the secretaries had never set foot in the technical workshops, even though some had been at the school a long time. They had only a notion of dust, dirt, grease and noise. To address this problem I organized a guided tour of the workshops with the help of the technical teachers and the pupils. They showed them how they were actually working. The visitors were astonished to discover computers, computer-driven machines, clean soil and pupils in white coats. Some teachers suddenly realized that they belonged to the same world. That helped a lot in future discussions.

The head teacher must resist the temptation to use a policy of divide and rule. This is the worst style of school management. Of course, you always find people with whom you have a better relationship and upon whom you can rely for support, but others should not gain the impression that they have been neglected. As an example, every term we have a class council where the teachers investigate the work of the class and individual pupils. Two parents and two pupils are also members of the council. The head teacher or one of the deputies takes the chair. I considered it a priority that I should chair every term's councils in each level of the school. This was a means of knowing every teacher and of making myself aware of the main problems faced by pupils.

Parents should feel real members of the school community, but communication with them is difficult sometimes. In the Lycée Lakanal we have three parents' associations represented on the school board and each association sends two representatives to these meetings. A monthly meeting is held between the head teacher and parent representatives. The meetings have no agenda. They are just an informal discussion about current issues at the school. I learn a lot and so do the parents, at least their representatives.

Explanations about the functioning of the school are given; we state why some decisions had to be taken and as a result the parents become more aware of the constraints under which we operate. Parents are then able to answer others when they complain about decisions and thus a better understanding is achieved. Suggestions for school projects can also spring from the meetings. One proposal helped those who lived far away and who could not be accommodated in the boarding school. The parents who lived close to the school found local private accommodation for the pupils.

French law requires the pupil to be in the centre of the system. Pupils learn more if they feel comfortable at school. One of the first things that we have to take care of is the quality of the equipment and building. The autonomy of the school, in this respect, allows us to undertake some work, but not major building programmes. Routine maintenance work, such as painting classrooms or corridors or the purchase of equipment like tables and chairs, is acceptable. However, pupils do not have the same sensitivity to their environment as adults. Many things that are shocking for us leave them quite indifferent. It is difficult to convince them that they have a responsibility for the school themselves.

We have launched many campaigns against graffiti and smoking in the school, which is officially forbidden by law. However, I must confess that we have not been very successful. On the other hand there is one thing to which pupils are very much attached. They call it 'democracy', but I prefer to call it 'fairness, information and a sense of respect'. It is clear that a school cannot be a democracy, since so much is decided centrally by the ministry. However, pupils need to be informed and consulted about facts and decisions in which they have a stake.

By law, pupils have to elect two delegates from each form at the beginning of the school year. The delegates constitute the council of delegates, which has to elect its representatives for the school board. Since 1999 schools have also been required to have a council of school life (Conseil de la vie lycéenne: CVL). The ministry has not yet defined its composition. All that is known is that it must consist of adults and pupils in equal number. This is something of a misnomer in our lycées because many pupils have already reached the age of majority and are lawful adults. I have decided to have 10 pupils and 10 members of the staff, but no parents. Amongst the staff are teachers, deputies, CPEs and members of the maintenance staff. It is important that pupils listen to the working conditions of all staff. A meeting is held every two months and the CVL tends to act as the organizing body of the council of delegates. Beside those important councils, pupils have representatives on many others that we also need. These include councils about public health, security and a committee for social and health education.

It is very important for the head teacher to help the councils to maintain their own life. He or she is a member of every council and has to spend a lot of time preparing the meeting, chairing, checking that minutes are taken and agreed actions are implemented. At the same time it is a powerful means of involving the members of the community in the life of the school. Everything can be said openly and discussed. If the decision is within the school's authority to take, everybody can give their opinion. Whether or not they agree with the outcome, they can be certain that the decision is not an arbitrary one. It is especially important for young people to be aware that there must be a debate before a yes or no is given. It is a lesson in democracy. If the decision is within the remit of the school, this can be explained together with a reason for the decision that has been taken. This too is a lesson of democracy.

Amongst the board's main tasks is the approval of the school project, discussion of the annual report from the head teacher and approval of the main internal rules. The main difficulty concerning the latter is to be sure that all agree what is meant by the rules and that they are consistently applied. The pupils are very suspicious about this aspect of school life and the head must be very cautious about this question. This is particularly so where punctuality and absenteeism are concerned. The pupils do not understand that, while they can be punished, apparently nothing happens to teachers.

Pedagogical role

Although in France the school, and therefore the head teacher, has no responsibility for the curriculum and final examinations, he or she is responsible for pedagogical life in general. The head must ensure that the teacher respects the curriculum, that regular homework is given, pupils are graded at the appropriate time and marks given to pupils. All these may seem trivial to teachers, but it is important for pupils and parents. If it is not done properly, pupils quickly feel that they are despised.

More particularly, the recent reform of the lycée, which is in its first year and concerns the first level, will have an important impact on future teaching style and therefore the organization of a teacher's work. In particular, those who take lessons with small groups of pupils will have to set personal work for pupils in two subjects. This will be difficult for our teachers who have not been trained in that style of teaching. The head will have to help them to organize themselves, to make teams of teachers and to choose the topics of the work.

Being a head teacher in France is a balancing act between managing centralized policy and leading individual, local initiatives. One must constantly remember that the compromises and the policies are all for the benefit of the pupils.

GLOSSARY

baccalauréat	Final examinations (age 18/19).
BTS	Brevet de technicien supérieur (diploma of higher education).
collège	First cycle of secondary education (pre-16): compulsory education.
CPE	Councillor for education (pupil discipline).
CPGE	Classe préparatoire aux grandes écoles: qualification equivalent to first two years of university.
CVL	Conseil de la vie lycéenne (council of school life).
lycée	Second cycle of secondary education (post-16): option of General, Technological or Vocational lycée or combinations of these (lycées polyvalents).

From vision to practice

CLIVE MINNICAN

Having left university in 1975, I spent two years working in a junior school in a socially deprived area of Ipswich. By 1977 I was ready for a move and was fortunate to find a post locally at Chantry Junior School, where I worked for six years. The school served a council estate largely occupied by hard-working families. I worked under a charismatic Welsh head teacher, Norman Brown, who was formative in the development of my leadership style. By gaining increasing responsibilities I was able to exercise leadership in a range of contexts. In 1983 I became deputy head teacher of a 600-place primary school working with an equally charismatic head, Roger Fern, now a Suffolk senior adviser. Roger was out of school on many occasions because of his wide-ranging responsibilities. This not only gave me plenty of opportunity to develop my leadership skills, but also the desire to exercise them in my own school. Four years later, in 1987, I became head of a 300-place junior school where I refined my leadership skills, learned from mistakes and clarified my vision. My current appointment followed in January 1994. I continued to extend my competence base through a wide-ranging involvement in broader educational activities. These included practising as an Office for Standards in Education (Ofsted) Inspector, a Lead Assessor for the National Professional Qualification for Headship (NPQH) and a trainer for the Ofsted school self-evaluation course.

SAINT MATTHEW'S PRIMARY SCHOOL

THE SOCIO-ECONOMIC CONTEXT

Saint Matthew's is a 150-year-old Church of England voluntary-aided school in the centre of Ipswich. The original school was demolished in the 1960s to make way for the inner ring road and a new building was erected on adjacent land. The school has grown to 340 pupils in 11 classes, with plans to extend to 14 classes enabling a two-form intake. The school is bounded on the east by the town centre, with large office blocks and the town market. To the north there is Victorian housing and a main arterial road largely fronted by small shops. On the west boundary there are several roads of large Victorian and Edwardian houses and, to the south, older high-density housing leads to the Ipswich Town football ground. Children from the locality come from a wide range of backgrounds, with parents from highly paid professionals to the long-term unemployed.

The socio-economic context is complicated by the fact that the school does not have a catchment area. Applications are judged against a set of admissions criteria, only one of which is residence in the ecclesiastical parish. Parental reasons for their choice include a variety of factors: the Christian faith, the school's uniform, the convenient locality, parental memories of the school and ethnicity.

During the 1950s, a large number of immigrants, many from St Kitts Nevis, settled in Ipswich and found a particular welcome at St Matthew's Church. This affinity for the Caribbean community extended to the school, and around 30 per cent of our pupils are of black or mixed heritage. Many travel across the town to attend school. This adds a unique dimension.

We are also regarded in the community as a good school. Many parents with high aspirations for their children are prepared to transport them several kilometres from outlying villages so that they can attend. The result is a culturally and socially diverse school, with the potential for this to be a source of richness and unity, or a cause of schism and disharmony.

THE SCHOOL IN 1994

My predecessor was a highly regarded teacher who had joined the school in 1983. His prime motivation came from working with children. He had found that the various changes through the 1980s and early 1990s diminished his job satisfaction, taking him away from the very aspects of the job he loved most. For this reason he chose to leave headship and return to teaching in another school. He continues to enjoy teaching and is active in St Matthew's Church.

I was selected at the beginning of the autumn term and so had three months to get to know the school before taking up my post. During that time an acting head teacher, Libby Brown, was very effective in preparing the ground for me. It was clear that there was a range of issues to be addressed.

Long-term plans were very sketchy and curriculum documents were either incomplete, old or absent. Documentation that did exist tended to be statements of policy with little practical application and offering no substantial guidance for organizing or teaching the subject. Furthermore, medium-term plans were very variable. There was no consistent format. Some teachers were reasonably thorough in their planning, whilst others seemed to have no plans at all. Similarly, assessment and record-keeping also lacked consistency.

The organization of the school mitigated against team planning. Classes were not organized into phase teams of parallel classes that could work together and teachers tended to work independently. The worst aspect of this organization was the 'transition class', which included children between the ages of 5 and 7 (Key Stage 1: KS1) and those between 8 and 11 (Key Stage 2: KS2).

The school development plan was skimpy, there was a clutter of unwanted equipment and furniture in many places and the staff did not want me there. I found out that, on the day of the interview, the staff were asked their opinion on the candidates for the headship. The feedback was that they did not mind who they had as long as it was not 'that Minnican person'. At least I was told that the budget was healthy.

On taking up the post in January 1994, I discovered that the budget was in fact heading for a £20,000 overspend. It was also apparent that falling rolls meant a drop in funding of a further £20,000 for the coming financial year. Within weeks of arriving I had to formulate a plan for saving £40,000 out of a total budget of around £380,000.

Other problems emerged during my first weeks. Friday afternoons did not exist for some children. I noticed that they could spend the time in the corner of the hall reading a comic, on the playground benches having a chat, or in the library playing chess. For some teachers this was simply what happened when children finished their work for the week. Staff disunity, bitchiness and gossiping in corners were endemic. Relationships were very poor. There was a culture in the school that whoever shouted loudest got what they wanted. This applied to staff as well as children. I had to deal with more incidents of bullying in my first month than in my previous year. Much of this bullying had a strong racist element and gangs of boys ruled the playground.

SIGNIFICANT CHANGES

The first change that had to be made was to tidy the school. I spent most of the Christmas holiday tidying up areas and putting up a display in the school entrance. I wanted teachers to come face to face with change when they returned in January. It became almost a standing joke that there seemed constantly to be a skip in the corner of the car park. This not only meant that the school became less cluttered, but it made the statement that things were changing.

I was soon in the fortunate position of being able to appoint a new deputy head teacher. The previous deputy took the opportunity to retire early. This was announced at my first staff meeting on the day before term started. The school appointed a deputy with commitment, tenacity to see a job through and strengths that complemented mine. For me, this was the dream ticket.

The school development plan had to be written. I chose to start this at the first staff meeting. I brainstormed all the things we wanted to see change. The rule was simple. Everyone had a right to speak and all ideas were to be included at this stage. A handbag hook in the staff toilet was as valid a contribution as rewriting the long-term curriculum plan. These ideas were placed on the staff room wall for two weeks so that people could add to them. Items were then prioritized at a second staff meeting and responsibilities allocated. Many of the trivial items had been completed in the meantime and could be checked off. Important items could then percolate to the top of the priority list.

The issue of bullying needed to be addressed early. This was done by insisting on the highest standards of behaviour at all times and by treating every incident seriously. Instant punishments, letters home to parents, meetings with parents and temporary exclusions rapidly restored a sense of order. It was hard work but it was worth it. One consequence of poor pupil behaviour had been that in one year group a significant number of parents had removed their children from school. This left a top infant year group with only 29 children out of a possible 49. This was a significant contributory factor towards the financial shortfall.

The staff wrote a behaviour policy. Three years later we reviewed this and decided to buy training in assertive discipline. We rewrote the policy in the light of this training and this produced a highly effective behaviour policy that is not only a paper document but is expressed in rules for the classroom, in the way teachers talk to pupils and in the procedures we follow automatically.

Curriculum documents had to be written in detail. It was important that these were addressed carefully and so they were included in the school development plan over a two-year cycle. The long-term plan identified a two-year rolling pro-gramme for the curriculum. It made sense for subject co-ordinators to write the long-term plan for their areas and then collate medium-term plans into schemes of work over a two-year period. This would have been fine if the National Curriculum had not changed with such regularity. At the end of the first two-year cycle there were significant changes and so we started again on the second two-year cycle. The staff skill at writing medium-term plans improved immensely over the first cycle and the revised set was far better than the first. The final stage has been to store these on computer disks so that teachers have rapid access in order to modify them in the light of evaluations or constraints.

I am committed to teamwork. When teachers are united in a task, sharing the responsibility and the workload, a synergy is released. This enables them to accomplish far more than if they had worked alone. It was clear that the organization of the school did not support teamwork. There were 'phase co-ordinators', but generally they did not understand their role. In KS1 there was a phase co-ordinator and a KS1 leader. These roles were in frequent conflict. The school was reorganized into three teams, called 'phases'. The upper phase comprised three parallel mixed age classes of 9- to 11-year- olds; the middle phase comprised a similar arrangement for 7- to 9-year-olds; and KS1 consisted of four classes, two of them mixed age and one early-years' class. I appointed a co-ordinator over each phase and gave them model agendas to help them in the early stages of leading phase meetings. Phase co-ordinators thus became the middle managers and, with the deputy head teacher and myself, formed the school management team. The team meetings followed the same model agenda as phase meetings and could be used as a model by the co-ordinators.

The quality of teaching was a key issue to be addressed. After a staff meeting, at which an advisor spoke on quality factors, a further meeting was held to discuss what we would expect to see in good-quality teaching. Teachers enjoyed this activity because it was close to their heart. They quickly identified issues such as well-planned lessons, clear objectives understood by pupils, well-prepared activities, a crisp introduction explaining the purpose of the lesson, good pupil behaviour management, an effective plenary session, good display, well-organized resources, and so on. This constituted our vision of good-quality teaching and forms the basis of our lesson observation programme. This in turn informs our system of appraisal.

Appraisal had not been undertaken in the school. It was seen as a bolt-on extra, rather than a useful activity contributing to the personal development of the individual teacher. It was clear to me that there was a range of activities that naturally fitted together. The school development plan is the key management tool. This is written in negotiation with teachers and subject leaders who produce their own sections. Lesson observations follow a regular programme, the purpose of which is to improve the quality of teaching. One of my early initiatives was to institute an annual dialogue with each teacher to discuss strengths, weaknesses, aspirations and support. These three elements were already fulfilling the performance management purpose of appraisal and it became a natural consequence to put them together in a staff development policy. The annual dialogue became the appraisal interview at which a teacher's strengths and weakness could be discussed. References to lesson observations provided a basis for parts of the dialogue and the teacher's personal aspirations helped to structure the training plan. The outcome of the dialogue is a written summary and an appropriate section for the school development plan. All teachers say they value this process. It has now been extended to all staff and phase co-ordinators undertake the dialogue with their team members.

One of my frustrations was the termly intake of 'rising five' pupils. Not only did this disadvantage a whole group of pupils, but it also caused organizational problems within KS1. Nursery vouchers were short lived but they provided the opportunity to start all pupils in the September before their fifth birthday. I am committed to early-years education and I was not prepared simply to admit pupils into a reception class. I used nursery voucher income to equip an early-years class, including the creation of an outdoor learning and recreation area. A KS1 teacher, who was trained in nursery education, had already been appointed. She was to be the guiding light in this initiative. A small working party was formed comprising the deputy head, KS1 co-ordinator, the nursery-trained teacher and myself. We spent several days looking at other nursery classes to learn from their strengths and weaknesses. The result is a highly successful early-years' class offering children the best possible start to school.

MAIN PROBLEMS DURING THE PERIOD OF HEADSHIP

Believe it or not, one of the major early problems was the staffroom table. The staffroom is small and was dominated by a large dining table. This meant that people on one side of the staffroom could not see, or talk to, people only a few metres away. It also meant that whoever was sitting at the table effectively held centrestage. This militated against staff unity and so I moved the table to the side of the room. This action generated some heated debate between several members of staff and myself. The table stayed at the side of the room! Meetings were much more efficient, lunchtimes more pleasant and the atmosphere more open. Above all, it signalled the fact that issues would not be avoided.

At the beginning of my headship there was a tendency among staff to prevaricate in order to avoid addressing issues. I wanted decisions to be made to a tight timescale. In order to achieve this, time limits were set. Staff meetings finish by 5 pm at the latest. If a staff meeting is held to discuss a policy, then the discussion is completed by 5 pm. I frequently use phrases such as, 'OK, let's move on' or, 'I need a decision on this…'. Before the end of the staff meeting I review what we have agreed without reopening the discussion. This is then written as a policy document that goes to the next staff meeting for confirmation before becoming school policy.

It was important to lay down the ground rule that we were looking for workable solutions. We were not to wait until we achieved perfection. This enabled us to develop approaches that could be implemented without prevarication. All policies had a review date so that weaknesses or problems could be addressed. I received very positive early feedback from this approach. Teachers felt that their time was being used effectively and they liked to see that decisions were being made. This strategy was one of the key elements in the change of culture at the school.

I had to be careful with the scale of the tasks to be accomplished. The school development plan has been absolutely crucial in ensuring that tasks were completed to a deadline. It is in my nature to want things up and running. I am not very patient. However, I am fully aware that school improvement is a journey rather than a destination and points on the journey need to be planned carefully. When the Ofsted inspection took place, the school did not have an information technology policy, but this was on the school development plan agenda for the following term. This planning process helped to overcome my frustration at not having things perfect immediately. The Information and Computer Technology policy may not have existed, but I could see when it would be in place!

The inspection was a bad experience. This was not simply because the teachers considered that they were being exposed in some way, but because our agenda was shifted. We had established a good pace of school improvement and we were doing this for ourselves. As a school we were learning to evaluate our work and how to make improvements. We were prepared to take risks and to experiment. We had wide horizons in our vision for improvement.

Then Ofsted came along. For several months the focus was shifted away from our own priorities and onto those of an external agency. I was so eager for a good inspection report that I allowed this to happen and took my eye off the ball. After the inspection the school developed what might be termed the POCS (post-Ofsted complacency syndrome), common to many schools during this period. We had spent several months clearly focused on the inspection process and it had become our sole vision. Now it was over and our vision had gone with it. I estimate that the inspection cost us a whole year in school improvement time. This consisted of six months in preparation and six months for recovery. I am determined that this will not happen again.

Finance was a real difficulty at first. The school had a falling roll and expensive staff. Staffing had to be reduced by one full time post and severe cuts made in all areas of expenditure. Some £20,000 had to be spent from reserves in the first two years. I marketed the school unashamedly, taking every opportunity for exposure in newspapers and on television. I dealt with all complaints personally. Nearly all, including incidents of bullying and racism, were dealt with the same day, preferably by personal contact or by telephone. If problems could not be sorted out that day, parents were contacted and told the reason. It is important for schools to value their children and parents. This builds confidence between the community and the school and adds to its reputation. The school roll started to rise again. It was, inevitably, some time before this led to an increase in funds. By taking hard decisions early the school avoided compounding the difficulties and we were able to enjoy the upturn when it arrived. We are now overcrowded in every class.

One notable failure has been the development of an effective assessment and record-keeping programme. Teachers have not valued any of the successive approaches. We have tried tick-sheets, mark books and computer records in various forms. However, the key to success is that teachers see this as a valuable activity. The various forms we have undertaken have been excessively bureaucratic and time-consuming, with no real advantage for the teacher. We are about to address this issue by asking the questions 'what do we want to assess, and how do we want to record these assessments?'

PRESENT STATE OF THE SCHOOL

The school is on a continuing path of improvement. The Ofsted inspection came just three years after I joined the school. It was a tough inspection and described us as 'an improving school'. It was clear that we were already better than 'satisfactory', but had not yet attained 'good'. The inspection came about a year too early. Nevertheless, school improvement is always on the agenda. Part of the programme of monitoring and evaluation is to identify ways in which we can secure improvement. A year ago we were awarded a Charter Mark for excellence. Applying for the Charter Mark was a valuable process that helped the staff to analyse the service we give and to identify ways in which we can improve. Arising from this, we began an annual survey of parents and pupils to ask our clients what the school is good at and what improvements are needed. The surveys often produce interesting ideas for improvement. This year we are working towards Investors in People (IIP) status. Again, this is a valuable tool for self-evaluation and has led to real improvements in managing professional development.

Teachers are highly motivated and there is a buzz of enthusiasm in the school. Staff morale is high and visitors comment on the positive atmosphere. This is surely due to the fact that school improvements have been carefully planned, avoiding overload and underpinned with a sound rationale reflecting the core business of good quality teaching. The result is a clear sense of purpose in the school.

APPROACH TO LEADERSHIP

My approach in underpinned by a range of values. I have a belief in the importance of our job as educators. It is essential to secure the very best for every pupil and to value the contributions from both pupils and staff. A punitive ethos or critical atmosphere is unacceptable, although I believe in setting goals and challenging underachievement. I believe in the strength of teamwork. A team is a group of people working towards a common end and enjoying shared success. This creates synergy and I believe in my staff. They are trusted to do a good job and I expect them to participate in decision-making. I am prepared to take risks and to be unconventional in looking for improved standards and I encourage these practices amongst staff.

I have a clear vision of how I want the school to be. Everyone in a school should understand the vision and its rationale. I also believe in using a range of strategies to attain the vision and in monitoring its implementation. This needs to be made clear to all members of staff and revisited regularly. At my first staff meeting I laid out my stall:

These are my expectations:

* work will be planned and prepared with work plans submitted early;
* curriculum plans and documents should be both detailed and useful;
* the school will be constantly reviewing and improving its work;
* rooms should be well organized, because this is our example to children;
* children will be interested in their work;
* children will be well behaved and courteous;
* sessions should start and end punctually;
* staff must be able to approach me immediately if there is a problem;
* staff will be supported and resourced as well as possible;
* the school will be the best in the county.

At a meeting of the governing body, led by the diocesan director of education, these ideas were developed into a school vision statement, 'The highest academic standards in a caring Christian environment.' The school management team then produced a parent information leaflet *We Have A Vision*, reviewed by the entire staff. This returned to the governors who decided that they should have a 'vision' working party, to ensure that it was implemented and did not remain as a paper exercise. We reconsidered our mission statement and identified the practical outworking of 'What does a caring Christian environment look like?' The working party set about producing a four-year school development plan. This not only meant that we spent several years repeatedly reinforcing our direction and reviewing its fitness for purpose, but it also ensured that governors were fully and appropriately involved.

Having established the vision for the school, it is necessary to spend time monitoring and observing the teaching, both formally and informally. I aim to spend some time in each class every week. This may only be a brief walkabout, but it ensures that the head teacher's presence in each classroom is noted. This gives teachers a chance to draw my attention to a child's work and for me to encourage them in return. There is also a programme of announced and unannounced monitoring against clear criteria, which I undertake with the deputy head teacher in accordance with the teaching and learning policy. Both oral and written feedback is given.

Clarity is very important. It is vital to know exactly what is expected of people. I try to avoid asking people to do unnecessary jobs. Teacher time has to be used effectively on purposeful activities that improve the quality of learning.

I challenge people who don't meet deadlines. If I ask for plans to be submitted on Monday morning and they are not there, I take the first opportunity to go to the teacher and ask why. The first time I did this I was asked, 'Oh, did you mean it? Only we haven't had to do this before.' In the same way, if a teacher has spent time writing plans, it is incumbent on me to give rapid feedback.

I try to maintain control of external pressures. As national and local policies appear and demands are made for their introduction, I plan the implementation (or rejection) according to the needs of the school. When new policies are published they can be divided into those to be implemented immediately and those that can be included in the three-year planning cycle. This means that the school is able to maintain its improvement agenda without being diverted by external pressures. There has been more than one occasion when, after careful analysis of the legal situation and of educational good practice, I have simply refused to implement a policy.

It is important to give clear criteria for decision-making and to insist that the criteria are applied so that the right decision is made for the right reasons. It is too easy to make decisions based upon what is expedient rather than what is right! On one occasion I needed to take two half-hour slots of classroom support time from a teacher to support special needs. I explained the reasons to the teacher and asked when would be the most convenient times. The teacher started to question me about whether someone else should lose his or her time, that no time would be convenient and that she had little enough time as it was. I restated that the decision was not whether I was going to take the time, but when this would take place. As the conversation continued, I pointed out that if the teacher was unable to make the decision, I would do so. After five more minutes I did. I make sure that everyone is clear about their role and I am prepared to stand firm if challenged.

I am prepared to challenge underperformance. Many head teachers find this a difficult task and many teachers will regard the slightest hint that they are under-performing as a personal attack on their professionalism. However, this does not need to be a painful process, provided everyone understands the agreed performance standards. For example, pupil behaviour management is a key aspect of effective teaching. If pupils' behaviour is ineffectively managed, then I will speak with the teacher about the expectations of the school and the reality of the situation. I will refer to real evidence of actual observations. 'When I was in your class I saw … I heard … Were you aware of that?' The aim is to engage in a constructive dialogue about how to improve performance. This inevitably puts pressure on the teacher, but by offering appropriate support it is possible to keep the focus on improving standards rather than personal criticism.

There are two other strategies that I adopt as the need arises. In order to support a member of staff, I work alongside to help them develop their own skill. I recently worked with a subject co-ordinator who was uncertain about lesson observation. Time was spent working through the lesson observation sheet discussing what each item meant. We observed lessons together and compared our notes. There followed discussion of the type of feedback that the co-ordinator could give. The co-ordinator is now confident in this role. Working alongside not only values staff, it empowers them and ensures that they do their job competently. However, this is a time-consuming strategy and can only be used selectively for developing long-term skills.

In order to achieve a short-term goal I may simply give orders. This is not a strategy I use a great deal as I am much more of an 'envisioner' looking to achieve long-term goals. However, if a simple task needs to be accomplished quickly, especially in an emergency, then giving orders and insisting on compliance is often the easiest way to get a job done.

Very rarely, I will take a job over if it is not being accomplished effectively. In this way I am able to maintain pace. This is a strategy that I do not like using because, although it may see a job finished, it has not addressed the underlying issue of time management or commitment. I prefer to intervene by working alongside other members.

In conclusion, I believe that to be an effective head teacher it is important to have a clear vision, to build a hard-working team and to monitor how the team is implementing the vision. We also have to be prepared for change. Over the last 18 months, two out of the 12 teachers have gained promotion to deputy head teacher and one to Key Stage leader. Only three teachers remain who were at the school when I started. It is, therefore, important to continually restate the vision, to monitor its implementation and maintain the drive for higher standards.

13

'Do we have to?'

MAUREEN CRUICKSHANK

After two terms of French and Russian at Oxford University, I changed to philosophy, politics and economics. In October 1963, with a degree and an engagement ring but no teaching qualification, I drifted into teaching French at an independent girls' boarding school. Marriage and five years in a newly opened comprehensive school, again teaching French, followed this absorbing one-year introduction to teaching. My three children were born during this time, when the norm was to give up your post after the birth of your first child. My decision to take maternity leave and return, initially full-time and later part-time, was viewed in many quarters with disapproval.

Work in primary schools and in a centre for English as a second language for secondary pupils and adults followed. My first big promotion was in 1973 to a house headship in Sidney Stringer, a multicultural inner-city comprehensive school in Coventry. Another brief house headship followed and then, in 1976, a deputy headship in a new Leicestershire upper school and community college. During 1973–75 I did a part-time Master's degree in education. I changed jobs and areas three times to fit in with my husband's career in education.

I wanted to get a headship before I reached 40. After quite a few applications and interviews the target was achieved with six months to spare. In April 1981 I became principal of the Beauchamp College, Oadby, Leicestershire, 5 kilometres from home, having spent over six years travelling at least 25 kilometres from home to work.

BEAUCHAMP COLLEGE

THE SOCIO-ECONOMIC CONTEXT

Beauchamp is a co-educational 14–19 comprehensive community college serving the community in and around a relatively affluent area to the south of the Leicester city boundary. Its catchment area includes rural communities. The school is over 600 years old, reputedly founded by Warwick the King-maker. There is an unbroken list of head teachers going back to the early 16th century. It had been a grammar school for boys in Kibworth some 6 kilometres away. After becoming co-educational it moved in 1964 to new buildings in Oadby and became fully comprehensive in 1968.

THE COLLEGE IN 1981

When I started, Beauchamp had 83 teachers and 1260 students taken from two feeder schools. It was one of the first schools in the county to become a community college and in 1981 had a community programme with over 1700 enrolled students and 57 affiliated clubs and societies. The sixth form of 380 was the largest in the county. The job details from the Local Education Authority (LEA) said: 'The school reflects its catchment area. The staying-on rate at 16+ is the highest in the county. The record of examinations is impressive.' The details also mentioned 13 mobile classrooms. The LEA forecast of numbers and staffing for the following eight years predicted that by 1989 the college roll would have dropped to 853 students with 55 teachers.

However, we maintained our student numbers, mainly by working hard at public relations and marketing. We have a file of press releases that goes back to 1991. We enjoy celebrating our success with the media and television companies seem to like filming us. Our lowest number on roll was 1000 in 1990 and it has increased steadily to 1850 students in 2000, with further rises anticipated.

MOVING BEAUCHAMP FORWARD

The curriculum

The first curriculum priority was to address the banding system. Before entry, students were allocated to three bands according to their ability. Each band had a highly differentiated curriculum. For example, only students in the top band could study music. So the bands went, to be replaced by a setting system. The first two years of headship were busy with many changes. However, during a stocktake of these changes, I suddenly realized that most items on the fairly long list were cosmetic and possibly had changed the college culture very little. It sometimes felt that it was still organized for staff comfort rather than for the achievement of student potential.

Organization and management

The dark days in 19 years of headship for me, as for most heads then in post, were during the union action and strikes in the mid-1980s. My instinct to fight, to contest, to do everything I could to remain open for students and to look after their interests, made my professional life during that period lonely and painful. Thankfully, a return to those circumstances seems unlikely. I am not sure I could manage that situation better if it were re-run. What was very important a year or so afterwards was to tear up the files, the memos, all the written material about that difficult time in order to bury the conflict and move forward.

We were one of the first Technical and Vocational Education Initiative (TVEI) schools and that experience of managing a small budget of our own helped us embrace Local Management of Schools (LMS) in 1990 with gusto. As part of our preparation for LMS, we went with heads of our feeder high schools on a return visit to a neighbouring public boarding school to see what we could learn from them about managing a budget. They had previously visited us to see our TVEI scheme in operation.

LMS gave us a leaner teaching force. Teachers are expensive resources and are best used in the classroom. Our aim was to release them from doing anything that could be done more economically and more efficiently by support staff. Today, support staff run all our examination administration, careers work, library administration and arrangements for cover for absent teachers. Each year-team of two-teacher year co-ordinators and up to 500 students has a full-time administrative assistant working in the year office. The assistant has considerable face-to-face contact with students. Faculties have their own administrative assistants and we have a General National Vocational Qualification (GNVQ) assistant who works with our 170 GNVQ students. We have an information and communications technology (ICT) team of seven technicians that includes a Web site manager.

In June 1998 we appointed a catering manager in preparation for running our own catering service a year later. Unfortunately, the Secretary of State decided to delay giving schools this opportunity until April 2000, which tried our patience somewhat. We were also a case study school in a Department for Education and Employment (DfEE) funded report on 'The Innovative uses of Non-Teaching Staff in Primary and Secondary Schools Project' carried out by the Institute of Education at the University of London in 1992.

Our leaner teaching force was achieved by natural wastage. We increased the size of our sixth-form teaching groups in line with similar increases in sixth-form colleges under the new Further Education Funding Council (FEFC) regime. The steady rise in student numbers enabled us to recruit excellent newly qualified teachers, especially during the economic recession of the early 1990s. We focused on improving the environment for students and staff. Mobile classrooms were removed and we undertook much new building, using funds from our own budget. We also set aside quite large sums that heads of faculties and departments could bid for in addition to generous capitation allowances. All of this contributed to a feel-good factor.

The most important ingredient in our current success, after creative management of the budget, has been our technology college status. We were successful at our third attempt to become a specialist college. The news of this success in December 1995 was a wonderful Christmas present. We had to raise £100,000 in sponsorship and present a bid that was acceptable to the DfEE. On 1 April 1996 the DfEE released to us £100,000 to match our sponsorship, together with £100 extra per student per year. The money has enabled us to provide world-class ICT facilities for staff and students. However, the main benefit of becoming a technology college has been that of finding a place through the Technology Colleges (TC) Trust in a group of schools that is 'can do', visionary, upbeat, and thinks the unthinkable, while maintaining a drive to raise standards. We have benefited enormously from the meetings and focus groups arranged by the TC Trust, which was the only educational body of its kind to survive the change of government in 1997.

We like the new emphasis, given after the United Kingdom general election in 1997, that requires specialist colleges to share 20 per cent of the funding with a family of schools and a further 20 per cent for work in the community. Our bid to renew our status in 1999 was accepted and we are now able to fund an ICT technician for the 10 schools in our family and to provide each school with additional computing equipment. We are also organizing master classes for some of their pupils.

Inspection evidence

We were one of the first schools to be inspected by the Office for Standards in Education (Ofsted) in September 1993. In our second inspection in May 1998, we were fortunate in having a registered inspector who recognized and celebrated our somewhat unorthodox approach. He told us we had challenged the dogma he walked around with, and that he had learned from us the importance of the question 'Do I have to?' The inspectors said they had never worked so hard or enjoyed themselves so much. Those on the team who still taught kept saying 'Why can't I teach at Beauchamp?' They told us that they saw exemplary teaching of a quality they had rarely seen before, with some sixth form teaching comparable to first- and second-year degree work.

Why did so many of our staff do so well? We have established a rigorous selection process for staff appointments. I believe that getting the very best teachers is one of the most important parts of my job. We analyse our staffing needs for the following year in late autumn and advertise vacancies in early spring so that we have the best choice of newly qualified teachers. Each teacher on interview is also interviewed by a panel of sixth-form students chaired by a member of staff. We ask all candidates to teach part of a lesson and we ask the classes they teach to give them marks and to write comments, with a particular emphasis on those who would get the best work from them.

Advanced skills teachers

Less than two weeks after our second Ofsted inspection we, like all specialist colleges, received an invitation to bid for significant funding for advanced skills teacher (AST) posts. Our Ofsted experience gave us the confidence to put forward a bid. We had two-and-a-half weeks to prepare! We bid for seven, one for each faculty. Two weeks later we heard that we had been given three, the maximum given to any school. This funding over two years covered start-up grants, costs of promotion and release for one day a week and amounted to £78,000 for the two-year period. Implementation involved preliminary interviews with staff interested in accreditation. We established with the DfEE that we could put forward as many teachers as we wished for accreditation, provided we bore the cost of the process for all but three. Any other AST posts we created would be funded from our own budget. Four ASTs were accredited in late August 1998 and took up post on 1 September. A fifth, a month later, and a sixth joined them in January 1999. During the remainder of that academic year, nine other teachers passed the accreditation and we gave each of them an additional half salary point in recognition of their achievement. One of these took up an AST post in September 1999, giving us seven posts in total, of which four are funded from our own budget.

The main benefit of our AST work has been the sharpened focus on our core activities of teaching and learning. More concrete benefits include our best ever examination results in 1999 at both GCSE and A level. Our A-level pass rate was a record 94 per cent, compared to a national pass rate of 88.5 per cent. Thirty-two of our 312 students who took A-levels got three or four grade A. These were excellent results as we operate a liberal entry policy to A-levels. However, we are not complacent. We know that our students and ourselves can do even better.

At GCSE in 1999, of our 451 students 69 per cent gained five or more A*–C grades, a rise from 67 per cent in 1998, which had been our previous record. Our pass rate in science increased from 61 per cent in 1998 to 68 per cent and in French from 61 per cent to 70 per cent. Our science faculty of 17 teachers has two ASTs in post and two others who have passed the accreditation. In languages there are two ASTs out of seven teachers, one of whom is in post.

All our ASTs are involved in mentoring students who are on the C/D grade borderline in general at GCSE and in particular within their subject specialism. All seven ASTs in post have been involved in outreach work in other schools, both within and outside our LEA. We have responded to all requests for assistance and consider it a privilege to help colleagues and to be enriched by experiences outside our own institution. We have put on a day's in-service training (INSET) on ASTs for three schools whose teachers wanted to visit us and have assisted with a Leicester University research project on ASTs. Each of our eight newly qualified teachers this year has an AST as a mentor and all the 30 postgraduate certificate of education (PCGE) students, who come to us as part of their initial teacher training, also has access to one or more AST. One of our teachers and an AST are now qualified Ofsted inspectors and another is part way through the training. These three staff say the training is tough and challenging, but is the best INSET they have ever had.

The feedback from the AST assessors to myself and the vice chair of governors in August 1998 identified what ASTs have in common. They have total commitment to, and respect for, students. Students find that ASTs are always available, they are never put down by them nor are they fearful of saying 'I don't understand'. They are also told what they will have learnt by the end of the lesson. The pace is fast. Students walk tall. They are a little in awe of the teacher and never quite know what to expect in a lesson. There is a tingle factor. Much of this had resonance with feedback from the Hay group's research work on teacher effectiveness in which we participated.

We welcomed the opportunity to nominate staff for the 1999 and 2000 Teaching Awards. In 1999 all five of our nominees, two of whom were ASTs, were regional finalists and two were regional winners. One of our regional winners, David Waugh, became the national winner of the best new teacher award.

Entrepreneurs all

At the end of 1999, we were one of 160 schools invited to bid to become a training school. The education department of a local university nominated us. The additional funding will provide £100,000 a year for three years. If successful, we will, in partnership with the university and with other schools, demonstrate and develop excellent practice in initial teacher training, explore and try out new approaches to the training of teachers and carry out and use teaching research.

We are all entrepreneurs. In 1999, after two years in post, our vice principal for community education had raised £175,000 for various community activities, the best known of which is our Spaceship. This is an ICT centre for the under-fives and is available for nurseries, playgroups, primary schools, parents and toddlers. It is now in continuous use.

We are active in bidding for additional funding and are perceived to be a wealthy college, even though we are 10th out of 17 Leicestershire upper schools in the funding we receive per student. Of course, not all our bids are successful. We hoped to become a centre for ICT training for teachers and were rejected twice. Other failures include some appointments and promotions that have been less successful than we would expect.

Curriculum innovation

We tend to be cautious with curriculum innovation. We watch others take the plunge and observe developments. I am forever grateful for the advice Duncan Graham, head of the National Curriculum Council, gave at the Secondary Heads Association (SHA) conference many years ago: 'Don't rush into anything too quickly'. And of course by the time the National Curriculum reached Key Stage 4, for 14- to 16-year-olds, it had changed beyond all recognition. Our primary school colleagues bore the brunt of all the unwieldy and over-complex initial stages. We add new A-level subjects – we currently have 36 – as and when we find that otherwise students would leave us to go elsewhere. GNVQ courses were first offered in 1995, a few years after they became available nationally. We are not at present making a major investment of staffing and other resources for key skills for post-16 students, in September 2000. We need to observe developments, particularly the emphasis which both the Universities and Colleges Admissions Service (UCAS) and individual admission tutors will give to such qualifications.

BEAUCHAMP TODAY

The college is flourishing with 1850 students on roll, of whom over 900 are in the sixth form. As a community college we achieved our aim this year to enrol 2000 part-time students in a range of 100 day and evening classes which are recreational, cultural and academic, but with a considerable emphasis on ICT classes. Our college aim is that 'Our students should become competent, caring young adults with the best possible qualifications, and that they should become lifelong learners'. Over 30 per cent of our students come from outside our catchment and 36 per cent of them are from ethnic minorities. More than 30 per cent of these are Asian, mainly from East Africa. This produces a wonderfully rich mix of cultures that we always seek to celebrate and affirm. We were proud of the statement in our last Ofsted report that 'the college prepares students well for the cultural diversity of contemporary Britain'.

For many years I was concerned that ethnic minorities were not well represented on our staff, at least in the same proportion as in the student body. However, when I mentioned my concern to a group of Asian business people whom I had been invited to address, I was told they had no such concern. It would be the least of their priorities.

For seven of the nine years since league tables have been published we have had the best GCSE results in Leicestershire LEA. League tables have been important for us. We are a non-uniform college, do not have a prefect system and do not present ourselves as highly academic. Before league tables were published, many were unaware of how good our results were.

BEAUCHAMP: LEADERSHIP ISSUES

The here and now

I often tell students in assemblies that I am haunted by the assertion, which I think came from the United States, that most human beings in their lifetime only achieve a small percentage of their potential. Our task at Beauchamp is to achieve as much of our potential, staff and students, as we possibly can. I also frequently tell them that we are all privileged to work at Beauchamp, and I mean it. I interview every one of 475 new entrants in the autumn term for 10 minutes, looking at their work and talking of, and hopefully sometimes raising, their aspirations.

The challenge over the years has been to raise staff expectations in relation to what students can achieve. A highly respected teacher told me, in all sincerity, a few years ago that we could not raise attainment any further. That was when our GCSE pass rate of five A*–C grades stood 10 per cent below what it is today. It is my belief that there are still considerable improvements to be gained. I am convinced that one of our greatest assets now is the expectation that 7 out of every 10 students who join us each autumn will two years later gain the qualifications they need to move on to post-16 advanced study.

Teacher expectation and student achievement

John MacBeath, in his lecture at the SHA Conference 2000, spoke of successful head teachers as being risk-takers with a healthy disrespect for authority. I have always had a rebellious streak as a pupil, as a teacher and as a head. Our registered inspector spotted that in our catch phrase 'Do we have to?' I want to encourage our students to be a little rebellious too, and part of the joy of being a head is that one is able to offer the rebel some protection against pressure to conformity. We aim for homogeneity between students and staff, sharing the same conditions of work and the same privileges. Our students deserve the best and most of all they deserve Carl Rogers' 'unconditional positive regard'.

We keep meetings to a minimum. Our senior management team of 10 meets weekly for an hour. All meetings have timed agendas and we use a system of process review to help us make the best of our time. This review has also helped enormously with meetings of the governing body. Governors' meetings are now usually one-and-a-half hours' long. We have few governors' subcommittees. The full governing body meets once a term and the finance committee six times a year. Vice principals' time, in my view, is better spent on raising standards than on the servicing of governors' subcommittees.

I very much welcome the increased accountability of headship that has happened over the last decade. We use benchmarking where we can, to see how we can improve, and we are not complacent. Examination results are analysed carefully and from many different angles. GCSE average student difference by subject and teacher, percentage pass rate for each subject A*–C, A* and A are compared with the national average for that subject and compared with the Beauchamp average across all subjects. Similar analysis takes place at A-level for top A and B grades. We study the average GCSE and A-level points score per subject from 1991 to the present, with supporting statistics from the LEA. Value-added measures are used to predict future success and we have charts showing the impact each GCSE and each A-level have on student and college performance.

Early in the autumn term we have faculty reviews, an hour with the head and deputy head of faculty, a vice principal and myself. A major topic is the examination results of the previous year. At the end of the summer term, a year before GCSE, the year office works out the probable pass rate together with the percentage of C/D borderlines. This is subsequently amended six months later. In the same term we collate predictions from faculties.

Every spring term I have a personal interview with all staff. Teaching staff give me their set lists, with value-added scores and predicted grades for GCSE and advanced level. My preparation for each interview includes careful comparison of the predicted grades with the value-added scores and I express concern if more than a handful of predictions are below these scores.

Four days a week we start the day with a 10 minute staff briefing. It is not always possible, but if we can laugh together during that time it makes a good start to the day. I try to be around the college at break, lunchtime and after school. I hope to be available and accessible to staff. Yet I clearly remember the words of a wise and experienced head teacher colleague when I took up headship: 'The staff room, Maureen, is like a jungle. The lions and tigers roar at you and the elephants trumpet. But if you can get through the jungle you come to quiet glades with rabbits and fawns. These quieter creatures are doing wonderful work.' The nurturing of talented staff is one of the great delights of headship. I try to remind myself frequently of the privilege of working with them and then celebrate their success as they move on to promotion elsewhere.

Looking ahead

We are aware of great changes facing schools in the immediate future as they embrace technological advances. We know that the fastest growing sector of education is home schooling. No nightmare school run and no problems with drugs or bullying. If schools do not adapt they will become dinosaurs. The Vision 2020 work of the TC Trust and SHA research on the school of the future are vital. We are sure that there will soon be much more emphasis on the way each individual student learns best, using for example Alistair Smith's work (1998) on accelerated learning in the classroom. We have several copies in college of *Emotional Intelligence* (Goleman, 1996). References to his work are increasingly frequent in the education world.

Scanning the environment includes the international dimension as we prepare our students for global citizenship. I value tremendously the opportunities I have had as the United Kingdom representative on the European Secondary Heads Association (ESHA), as a SHA speaker at the Australian Principals' Conference in Melbourne in 1994 and as a member of the Indian Public Schools Conference in Arunachal Pradesh on the Chinese border in 1996. Our students are going further and further afield. Australia beckons in 2000, including a home stay with our partner school Bendigo, Victoria. We have had a ski trip to United States and a rugby tour of Canada is scheduled. There has been a food trip to China, not to mention World Challenge expeditions to Mexico and Borneo. During one half term I took two sixth-form students on a visit to a school in South Africa. We have the usual exchanges with France and Germany and an annual sixth-form water sports holiday in the south of France.

But what of the head teacher's 'hinterland', as Dennis Healey put it. What nurtures and re-energizes the head and brings perspective, ideas, and creativity? For me nature, getting out of a ski lift in the sunshine and looking down the valley. Flexing the muscles for the exhilaration of a run; or standing at the top of Helvellyn or one of the Munros; sunrises and sunsets anywhere in the world; also family, friends, good books, plays at Stratford, and opera. We neglect our hinterland at our peril. I say each year to the delegates on the course I direct for SHA 'Women into Deputy Headship' that workaholics are usually rather boring, often stressed and uninspiring. I always quote to the delegates the four qualities I heard Tim Brighouse identify as the essential qualities of headship: intellectual curiosity; regarding crises as the norm and complexity as fun; an unquenchable sense of unwarranted optimism; and a complete absence of paranoia or self pity.

The Ofsted report in May 1998 said: 'The governors, principal and senior management team provide strong leadership and have a good capacity to reflect critically on all aspects of the work of the college and convey a clear sense of purpose.'

What is important for me is the critical reflection. We know we can do better. And we have fun.

REFERENCES

Goleman, D (1996) *Emotional Intelligence*, Bloomsbury, London

Smith, A (1998) *Accelerated Learning in the Classroom*, Network Educational Press, Stafford

Flanders swansong

PAUL DESMET

After starting as a teacher of languages and history I first became a head teacher in 1968. To be appointed head of a girls grammar school was an unusual step for a lay person. Invariably it would have been a priest in the Catholic church. There I have remained, but my own learning has continued through a variety of opportunities. Study visits throughout the EU and beyond have contributed to a wide understanding of leadership. In 1985 I became the first president of the Flemish Secondary Heads Association, spending some time as the Flemish representative on the EU education committee. Since the early 1990s I have represented Belgium on the board of the European Secondary Heads Association (ESHA).

LYCEUM O.L.V. TER – NIEUWE-PLANT, IEPER

In Flanders, the northern part of Belgium, Dutch is the mother tongue and foreign languages are at the very centre of the secondary school curriculum. Since the 16th century when state and Catholic Church became synonymous, Flemings have tried to circumvent the laws because they have never been made for the

Flemish people, but were used by foreign powers, or the French-speaking aristocracy, to improve their own wealth and glory.

In the new independent state of Belgium, a country since 1815, language has never been a unifying cultural force. The dialect-speaking Flemings in the north, faced with the superior French culture and industry in the south, had a long journey of emancipation in front of them. Compulsory education was the key breakthrough in the second half of the 20th century. Before I realized it, I ended up in that emancipation process as head teacher of a Catholic grammar school for girls. Ironically, I was invited to take up the post by someone who had been my own head teacher when I was a student. I asked him for three weeks to think it over. I had to come to terms with leaving my job as a teacher of Dutch, German, English and history. How could I do that? Would I still have enough time to read? That was my immediate response.

Anyway, I jumped into the unknown. I could not imagine what the head teacher meant by a 'fairly good class grammar school for girls' but I soon found out. The nuns in the convent associated with the school preferred to speak French. They considered themselves to belong to the better part of society, though the pupil intake came from the lower middle and middle classes and from the farming community of the generally rural environment. I was fortunate that I did not know anybody in that part of the province. Before I started, the local head inspector told me: 'I'm giving you 10 years to make a school out of it.' I did not understand what he meant at the time. Flanders has no national assessments. Therefore there is no way of comparing schools by results and the variation in academic performance between secondary schools is enormous. In Flanders, only 49 per cent of the students pass the examinations in their first-year at university. In my school, however, over the years we trebled the number of those passing their first year university examinations, now a figure of 82 per cent. I made a school out of it!

After years of discussion, my single-sex school became co-educational. We still have mixed feelings about it. It would have been easier had we been able to start with a new school on a new campus. The former boys' school attracted more girls than the girls' school did boys. Choice does not seem to be so much a matter for parents any longer. More and more of their 12-year-old offspring decide to which school they will be going. Now only 25 per cent of our students are boys. Whether a co-educational school is better than a single-sex school, I could not say.

HEAD TEACHERS, THE CHURCH AND THE STATE

Headship, just what does it mean today? The question 'what is a head teacher expected to do?' has kept returning to me over the years. When I took up headship, I knew more or less what a Catholic school was supposed to be. About 75 per cent of the secondary schools belonged to the Church, although they could not be too Catholic. Their high quality and long tradition stems from the priests, monks and nuns who have played a dedicated role in Flanders education over the ages. The Church invested money in school buildings and preserved the freedom to educate and, where possible, to indoctrinate the younger generation.

When in 1968 I told one of my colleagues that I had accepted the headship of a Catholic girls' school, he reacted in bewilderment. He said, incredulously, 'How can the church authorities do that? They cannot appoint lay people in a grammar school!' As the first lay person to become the head teacher of a Catholic grammar school in West Flanders I was, to begin with, uneasy when head teachers got together. For a long time I had the feeling that I was just about tolerated. Even today, you can hear important clerics talking about the evolution of secularization that, in spite of all their efforts, they had not been able to prevent. Anyway, in 1968, 99 per cent of headships in Catholic schools were still in the hands of religious people. Today it is the other way round.

It was not always easy for a lay person to be in charge of a Catholic school. The clergy had always been used to following the instructions of their authorities and it was taken for granted that we would do the same. By the end of the 1970s, they started noticing that this was not the case, and Church members of the school board came 'to help me'. As proprietors of the school buildings, they can still intervene in the management of their schools.

So it was in 1998 that the Church ordered Catholic schools in the Flemish community, through the Flemish school boards, to implement the structural changes that it had proposed. Hardly any school wanted them, but the Church won. As a head teacher, I could never have received a harder slap in my face, but I knew that the next day I had to start preparing the new structure in a constructive way.

LEARNING FROM OTHERS

I was a head teacher who had read articles about what a democratic school should be like. I had visited comprehensive schools in Leicestershire and Sweden, and come back still not convinced. 'Should children ever be kept back? Can education be good if the full potential of youngsters is not met? Do we have to treat all the 12-year-olds in the same way? Can schools be used for specific political options?'

My critical attitude of dogma resulted from looking behind the scenes. I visited Countesthorpe Community College in the UK, read about growing discontent with the one-sided ideological approaches of the school system and spoke to parents in the Malmö City Hall in Sweden, whose world collapsed under the interfering welfare state. 'Of course, there are excellent comprehensive schools, but to expect all schools to become comprehensive is simply too directive,' I thought. What schools should be about, whatever their type, is enhancing the development of each individual child throughout their school career.

Having no career ambitions myself, I never had to put up a façade. Together with a friend of mine, I wrote a book about what I believed to be right. Articles concerning education and school systems followed. I gave talks wherever I was asked. The gist of it all was, repeatedly, that there is no final answer to the question 'what is the best educational system?' No single system should be forced upon pupils, parents and teachers. In the end, it is the pupils' final results that count compared with where they started. The best innovations are those that head teachers and teachers believe in. We do not need politicians and church people telling us in detail what we have to do and how we have to do it. We only need the state to decide the amount of money available for education and how to distribute it. The state should respect that we in education are trained and experienced professionals.

Being responsible professionals is difficult in a system that is becoming ever more prescriptive. In Flanders, the authorities believe that detailed plans have to be produced by each school to be able to cope with its responsibilities. All meetings have to be reviewed. Reports have to be made to the inspectorate. The 'nanny-state' is exploding into ridiculous proportions! Never in the history of the Flemish region has the department of education published so many decrees about every aspect of school life, prescribing even the way in which pupils, teachers, parents and the local community are expected to participate in the education process.

It can only be in Flanders where schools have not been able to run their own personnel management systems. A teacher who acquires rights in one school has automatically the same rights in any other. Teachers who are part-time have priority in all the schools of the region to extend their job into a full-time post. Parents have the right to sue the school if their child has not passed examinations. We live in a litigious world.

All the orders do not leave much space for Belgian head teachers to assume responsibility. Many are demoralized or are reaching the danger zone of defeatism and indifference. The majority does not stand up for its beliefs. 'We have done what is officially expected and that is it!' all too often becomes the motto used by new head teachers in order to survive. Instead of allowing heads and teachers to pursue the processes that lead to quality education, the state meddles more and more in our daily activities, robbing us of the creativity we need. Head teachers do not have the freedom or the time to think critically about their job. When 15 years ago the newly founded Flemish Secondary Heads Association chose me as its first president, it was considered a rebellion against the authorities. I used to tell my younger colleagues that they would not be undertaking their responsibilities properly if, in some cases, they did not challenge the system.

HEAD TEACHERS AND THEIR SCHOOLS

Head teachers will not become demotivated if their moral and humane leadership inspires and stimulates teachers and their pupils. After 20 years of experience as a head teacher, I told my colleagues: 'We are the navigators, confident in what we are doing, but never arrogant or boastful. Sometimes we have to sail against the current, hovering through the waves and between the rocks. Every man goes to his own gods by his own road.'

Maybe the school I led for more than 30 years would not have been what it turned out to be if their head teacher had not trusted the staff. Nor if they had not had the opportunity to find out for themselves what they considered to be good or if they had not been stimulated to go 'to their own gods by their own road'. Their reputation with parents and the results of former students in higher education have always been considered far more important than any bureaucracy.

Staff need to be given freedom, even if their ideas are doubted. 'Yes, of course, that would be nice!' has often been my reaction to an initiative proposed by staff members. I cannot but appreciate their readiness to try out something new, their common sense and experience. When they called a meeting to present a project to their colleagues, I go and listen, but hardly ever utter a word except perhaps, 'That sounds very interesting. Please, go ahead. I don't care what the inspectors might say!' Some months later at an evaluation of their project, when I have heard them say that their idea had been a mistake, I might say, 'We are all learning! If we cannot make mistakes, let's dig a grave and go and lie down in it. I love mistakes of that kind because they show that we are doing something.' In a school beehive, some workers will make mistakes!

As a head teacher I have hardly ever been angry, though I have been nervous at times. Some five years ago, while preparing an information session for 12-year-olds and their parents, a teacher remarked quite harshly that it was time to turn these sessions into pleasant events for the children. He believed in the philosophy that children should be given what they want and not what they need. I retorted that it was my conviction that these sessions had, in the first place, to be informative and of high quality and that these aims were not going to change for the time being. I am familiar with child-centred education. Common sense prevents me from believing, however, that becoming infantile is the way to the future.

I have never liked the teddy bear, rucksack and lollipop culture among 16- to 18-year-olds. Whenever they come to ask me permission to do something, I like to throw the ball back into their own court to make them decide. They smile when I tell them, 'You are clever and grown up enough. I have no doubt that you will make the right decision and that you will be ready to live with the consequences.' In many cases, we should let them find out for themselves and draw their own conclusions. As a head teacher or a parent I have never believed in taking away their responsibility or in bending over backwards to please them. Some staff members do not see any harm in spoiling these tender, sensitive children. There is a tendency in educational circles to expect teachers to help children as soon as there is something they do not understand, or as soon as a problem arises. The expectation is that we should solve it, not the pupils. By keeping problems away from students, not expecting them to find their own solution, we achieve exactly the opposite of what we are aiming at. We do not let them grow up.

PARENTS AND SCHOOLS

Some time ago, I visited a school in Berlin where I talked to the head teacher, some teachers and the school social worker. His green punk hairstyle and heavy-metal collar must have prevented me from counting his rings! On the other hand, was it because he made me think so much? Was this social worker trying to be one of the youngsters? Was he giving signals of wanting to make up for what he had missed? When he mentioned that he had never known his father, I thought of modern parents who have no time for the education of their children. Could their priorities, such as their own freedom and personal development, in some cases stand in the way of their children's development? Why has violence in schools become such a problem? Why is it in Belgium that we are now having special in-service courses on communication problems, drug abuse, motivation, child abuse, aggression and criminality? Everything is given over to the hands of experts and different institutions. Are we becoming a society without parents?

Yet, I have always liked the parents' association. Meeting with them five times a year has made me realize that in some cases they know better than I do what is happening at school. I keep on listening, learning, answering, reacting and letting them publish their reports in the school newsletter. When they started suggesting teaching methods, better than those used by the teachers, or looked down on teachers 'who have so many holidays', I started getting nervous. There is a strange paradox nowadays. Parents invest less time, love and warmth in their children's lives, yet at the same time expect more from the teachers and even give us advice on how to do our job!

Are we in schools providing the younger generation with a good service if we become the repair shops for everything that is going wrong elsewhere? Do we really need more specialists? When, with the help of the media, the bulldozer is rolling, telling heads and teachers how we should behave, what we should think and what priorities we should have, can we stop or ignore it? If values and citizenship do not stem from parents, the developed world will be heading for one of its most problematic periods. As far as schools are concerned, parents are usually grateful if their children are taught to work hard and to take responsibility and if they are well prepared for higher education. Deceiving parents is a crime.

LEADING SCHOOLS

Today, we need motivated heads and teachers who are trusted and recognized by society to take the lead in their students' development. No course for future head teachers can prepare a person for learning the job better than actually doing it. Finding solutions through trial and error, figuring out the best possible solution, creates motivated and responsible head teachers. You learn and grow in the job by looking and listening, falling and standing up again. I would not have had it otherwise. When in the 1980s I was involved in in-service courses, younger head teachers and deputies used to ask me where I learned my job. 'I sometimes wonder,' I answered, 'maybe I approached my job a little bit as an outsider, always maintaining a bit of distance.' Whatever the regulations coming from Brussels, I ask the question. Is it the best thing for the pupils, the parents and the teachers? I often got away with it, but sometimes, whatever my convictions I have had to follow the instructions.

'How on earth is it possible to remain a head teacher in this political climate in the same school for more than three decades?' is the question I am always asked. I say, 'Use your common sense! Keep smiling; talk to parents who sometimes act as an excellent sounding board. Don't let the business community tell you how teachers should teach. Encourage youngsters. Ask for some help from the guy you clashed with the evening before. Face the problems, but get around the obstacle when necessary. Above all, take new initiatives.'

Colleagues in other countries have greatly influenced my school leadership. Since 1970, I have visited many schools abroad, mainly in Europe, but also in the United States, the former German Democratic Republic and Israel. There are no countries in the European Union (EU) where I have not taken part in study weeks and seminars. In addition, because in different countries different answers are given to the same questions, I not only came back with new ideas but also started broadening my views on education, asking fundamental questions and returning to basic principles.

I can no longer imagine leading a school without some comparative experience.

Since I consider education the most essential responsibility of every society, I have told parents and teachers repeatedly that we educators have an extremely important job. Head teachers do not need to be specialists or experts, following the advice of universities or feeling incompetent when exposed to scholars' resounding articles with impressive footnotes. It is enough to be people with a heart, with a belief and a conviction, with the innate desire to stimulate student interest and an appetite for life. Educators are there to create an environment where it is good for all children to be and to give priority to those among them who are in need.

I was quite happy some years ago to have my career as a head teacher interrupted for 16 months to assist the ministry of education to prepare for the presidency of the EU and to be the Flemish representative on the EU education committee. When, however, at the end of that time I was invited to stay, I did not consider it for one minute. I wanted to go back to my small town, get on my bicycle in the morning and go to school. There I could meet the real people and be faced with youngsters with great expectations and a willingness to trust, respect and listen.

For about six months, I found myself thinking about a new European project to bring students together from EU schools. The first meeting for staff of the new school year would be the right moment to say something about it I thought. That proved to be a mistake. I should have known that, in a full staff meeting, teachers are sceptical. Anyway, since I believed completely in my idea, I worked at it. What a delight it was to see my dream gradually grow into the most astonishing project of my career. Now, every year, six schools from six different EU member states meet each other with 120 pupils for a well-prepared study week in March. The students are ambassadors for their school and their country; all of them speak a foreign language. 'The best thing that ever happened in our school' said one of the teachers with whom I had been working for a quarter of a century.

FINAL THOUGHTS

I was discussing broad human issues of truth, religion and politics with a good Jewish friend of mine some years ago in Jerusalem. At one point, he said, 'How could we ever pretend to have found the truth or to offer definite solutions? Whether we are Christians, Jews or Muslims, we have all grown up in a specific environment with its own traditions, beliefs and values. But since the Messiah has not arrived yet, we are always looking for new and better answers to the many questions we are faced with.' He made me realize that I believe that a good school will have at its heart values, conviction, belief and integrity.

Conclusion

This book demonstrates the rich variety of styles of school leadership. There is no single way to lead a successful school. While much depends on the character and experience of the head teacher, the time and place is also important. The context and history of the school are factors that no successful head ignores. There is then, no straightforward answer to the question posed at the end of the Introduction, 'What makes a school leader successful?' There are, however, some common themes in the chapters and these form the basis for this concluding section.

The changes in the nature of school leadership during the last 20 years of the 20th century were greater than in any comparable period of time. The most significant was the move from central direction of the work of schools to a much stronger role for the school itself in the management of resources. Several of the heads in this book have pointed to this change as a watershed, bringing a range of new problems and opportunities in the leadership of schools. Many UK heads have found that the Local Management of Schools (LMS), while providing a welcome increase in financial autonomy, has brought even greater benefits in the accompanying management freedom. School leaders and governing bodies have been able to develop their own appointment procedures and have no longer needed to refer decisions on a wide range of issues to local authority officials. On an international front, Jarvis comments that site-based management energized the leadership of her school in Colorado, providing the potential for new and radical developments that served the needs of her school community. For Peachey, the introduction of bulk funding in New Zealand was a turning point that brought many opportunities for school improvement, after the initial problems had been overcome. In contrast,

Sackur expresses the limitation felt by school leaders in France who have little autonomy over resources and staffing. In Flanders, the centralization of decision-making by Church and State and the lack of trust in school leaders has not only frustrated heads such as Desmet, but has robbed school leaders of the capacity for creativity that provides the excitement and reward for so many head teachers in other countries.

Several chapters have explored the differences between leadership and management and point to the need for both to be effective if a school is to be successful. Plant observes how a school-based management scheme can cause head teachers to spend too much of their time in managing school resources and consequently relax their leadership in vital areas such as curriculum and pedagogy. Several contributors illustrate how an early emphasis on the primacy of teaching and learning can be an essential element in refocusing the work of a school. After a period in the early 1990s, when head teachers gave a high priority to the new challenges of school-based management, successful school leaders have turned their attention more towards pedagogy and the outcomes of teaching. Greater public awareness of school examination results has increased pressure on school leaders to ensure that teaching and learning are successful and this has led to a widespread increase in structured lesson observation.

The essence of leadership is in setting the vision for a school and empowering others to drive towards the fulfilment of that vision. As Plant states, there is no leadership without vision, but Nicholls points out that the vision is rarely acquired on the road to Damascus. Many chapters illustrate how a vision, underpinned by a clear philosophy of education, creates an ethos that characterizes the school and its leadership style. The more difficult part of leadership is to transform the structures and practices of the school in a way that transmits the vision into the everyday reality of school life. Several contributors comment on the need to involve members of the governing body in the formation of the vision. Others developed the vision in a collaborative way with staff, students and parents. Where the enactment of the vision trespassed on to the hallowed ground of established practice, the process of winning support became more difficult and compromises had to be struck, as recounted by Peachey when government decided to bulk-fund the salaries of teachers. This illustrates the need for openness in discussing proposals for change, although the setting of the initial vision may be a more autocratic process, especially where a school staff has become complacent, as Bennett found when he started his second headship. Even then, he listened carefully to staff, and incorporated many of their views, before declaring his hand.

Those for whose work they have just become responsible watch new leaders carefully. Early decisions are dissected for signs of what may be to come. The impact of these early decisions is considerable and several contributors chose an issue on which to make an early statement. Hardacre's removal of the staff sign-ing-in book signalled his belief in the professionalism of the teachers. Doig's scrapping of hundreds of old chairs and tables illustrated the potential benefits of the school's newly devolved budget and established his reputation for action. Pritchard employed a scrap merchant to clear the detritus from the school before beginning to decorate it himself. These apparently trivial examples were each important in the context of the school and helped to pave the way for more sub-stantial changes. In situations where the school is not performing well, decisions may be taken that show an early determination to tackle a problem of central importance. For Minnican, the issue was bullying; for Hardacre, it was teaching quality; for Clough, it was the relationship between the senior and junior parts of her school.

The impact of these decisions outweighed their importance, in that they pro-vided early examples of the leadership style of the new head. No leadership style is likely to be permanent, however, and may change according to circumstances. Fawcett notes how he adopted different styles for different situations, moving, perhaps in the course of a single day, from a consultative approach in policy development to an autocratic response in an emergency. Bennett made a deliber-ate decision to lead a complacent staff from the front in order to make early progress and then moved to encouraging from the rear, when others had shown themselves capable of change management. Effective leaders develop a variety of modes of leadership and must be conscious of the possibilities created by the use of a range of styles. Less important than the perceived single style of a leader is the ability to match the style to the occasion.

Moving from one leadership style to another implies a degree of risk and, as Cruickshank and Nicholls note, effective heads must be risk takers. Desmet and Minnican argue that staff, as well as head teachers, must also be allowed to take risks. The growing accountability of heads and, through them, the teachers is sometimes at the expense of creativity and risk taking. This is especially true in schools, such as Hardacre's and Plant's, which serve disadvantaged communities. In these schools, performance indicators often look worse than other schools and concentrate the minds of head and staff on the central task of improving exami-nation results. It takes a courageous head teacher to adopt risky solutions in this situation. Only when central authorities devise fairer performance indicators, tak-ing account of the prior attainment and socio-economic background of the stu-dents, will this be remedied.

The aims of all schools are broad, going well beyond examination results and always including the personal development of young people, as much as their aca-demic attainment. Whatever performance tables may show, school leaders will often say that their greatest satisfaction comes from the creation of opportunities for the personal development of young people. Desmet cites the six-country European exchange project that he founded and which has had a significant impact in all the participating schools, including his own. Cruickshank's entrepreneurial approach to government initiatives has brought benefits to her school. Structural opportunities, such as specialist college status and advanced skills teachers, have helped to release student and teacher potential. Jarvis mentions 12 foreign exchanges in her school and projects such as adopt-a-senior and the immersion programme, which created cultural and academic opportunities for students. By no means all the innovations in schools come from the head teacher. Successful heads create a climate in which other staff and pupils can propose and implement change. This enabling leadership style 'holds a space open for others to emerge', comments Jarvis (quoting Wheatley), and helps to release the energy of talented teachers.

The management of change is a subset of leadership and is best seen in the context of transmitting a leader's vision into reality. Change is rarely popular, although heads generally find a constituency of support for their proposals in at least part of the staffroom. New heads who meet with every member of staff to hear their concerns, as Bennett did, have a clear picture of where support and opposition are most likely to be found. Minnican soon discovered this by relocating the table in the staffroom, both as a symbolic and real change at an important time. Resistance to change may come from an unwillingness to move from a zone of comfort and reluctance to shoulder responsibility, as in Bennett's school, or from other historical and cultural factors. Nevertheless, building the capacity for change is at the core of leadership. *Status quo*, as Hardacre observes, is not an option for any school, least of all schools like his, serving challenging communities. Pritchard has a school management plan that is constantly being updated and is never regarded as definitive. Fawcett states, as all the others recognize, that continuous development is necessary if a school is to sustain improvement.

'Walking the talk' is an expression that has gained currency in recent years to describe the need for a leader to be in close contact with the work of the school and to observe the effects of policies and practices on young people and their teachers. Jarvis quotes Covey on the need to 'seek first to understand'. Clough adapts Keats in wanting to 'feel the school around me', while Peachey frequently walks around the large school and Plant likes to spend time 'talking the vision' to key individuals. Doig recognizes the importance, not only of the head absorbing what is happening in the school, but of the power of the head's presence to influence directly the work of students and teachers.

Many people find headship a lonely job and leading change can be an uncomfortable experience. Increasingly, however, the leadership of schools is being shared amongst a group of senior staff, usually known as the senior management team. Nicholls considers that the best leadership comes when the members of the team share values and goals and challenge with each other constantly. The term leadership group is becoming more widely used, especially in England and Wales, where a new salary structure has introduced a leadership pay spine for heads, deputy heads and others with strategic responsibility across the school. All chapters have considered the nature of shared leadership, extending beyond the immediate leadership group to team leaders, and empowering the maximum number of staff in the enactment of the vision. This goes a good deal further than participation in decision-making. It encompasses a responsibility for the establishing and execution of policies. Higher levels of corporate and individual responsibility can be built on a collaborative approach to problem solving and policy development. Minnican notes that this requires the head to 'believe in the staff' and, where this happens, Fawcett's principle of subsidiarity can be applied. In the field of pedagogic leadership, all must be involved. Bennett and Doig recognized this early in their headships and ensured that members of the leadership group held significant responsibilities for teaching and learning which, in many schools, have traditionally been delegated to team leaders. Direct involvement of the head teacher in monitoring teaching and learning is seen as important. This sends a clear message to all concerning the importance of the quality of the learning experience. Learning is the core activity of the school and cannot be monitored solely through a study of statistical output. Schools are, however, becoming increasingly data-rich institutions, as they strive to measure their work and to compare performance year on year. Inheriting the headship of a mixed school in which many classes were taught in single-sex groups, Nicholls developed sophisticated systems of data-gathering in which analysis of the performance of sub-groups (gender, subject and ability) provided evidence of the added value and drove his school's improvement.

Many leaders feel strongly the tension between internal and external pressures. Minnican expresses the need to balance internal and external influences. The leader acts as a sieve for external initiatives and constraints, only allowing through the sieve those that are of potential benefit to the school and which will not distract it from its declared purpose. He notes how an Ofsted inspection had shifted the school's agenda and estimated that this had cost a whole year in school improvement time. Other external pressures, often resulting from government initiatives, can hinder the progress of schools. Plant's multi-age reform programme was impaired by the conflicting priorities of successive state governments, causing frequent changes in the way schools were managed. In several countries, head teachers found that the policy of open enrolment, in which parents are able to express a preference for the school they wish their child to attend, created the need for marketing the school. Although this produced an additional workload and an unintended change of direction, Hardacre found that an active marketing policy in the local media had positive benefits for the school and its community. It gave public recognition to those whose achievements would otherwise have gone unnoticed. In a community with low self-esteem, good publicity can make an important contribution to the development of a culture of achievement. He also found that closer co-operation with the local police produced tangible benefits, not only for the school, but for the whole community. The benefits of external links sometimes seem peripheral and a cost-benefit analysis in this field is not always encouraging. Fawcett is clear about the benefits, but notes how easily external links can fail and how they need to be constantly developed.

Considerable thought is given by school leaders to the way in which governors can best be used. Heads have to adopt a range of strategies in order to ensure that individual governors are well informed, and that the demarcation line between the strategic and accountability role of the governing body and the leadership and management role of the head and senior staff is clearly understood. From Clough's account, it seems that the division of responsibilities may be clearer in the independent sector.

Schools also put a great deal of work into forging positive links with parents. Pritchard shows how the head of a small primary school can benefit from direct, daily contact with parents. Sometimes the close involvement of parents can bring unwelcome pressures, as Jarvis found when proposals generated by parents threatened to divert the school from the route which it was taking towards its agreed goals. More often, heads agree with Sackur that good communications with parents are vital if the achievements of students are to be maximized.

The importance of communications, both within the school, and between the school and the community, cannot be overestimated. Leadership, as Jarvis states, may be action and not position, but effective leadership is 10 per cent action and 90 per cent communication. The reputation of the school may be enhanced by good communications, but these can be no substitute for effective policies and successful outcomes. The heads in this book are all still searching for the best route to success, the key to unlocking the potential of students and teachers, and are constantly urging their staff to do the same. As Nicholls states, good heads never stop thinking and listening.

The changes to school leadership in the first 20 years of the 21st century may well be greater than those on which this book has reflected. The school of the future is likely to be a learning centre for the local community, open all hours, in which young people and adults complement their other learning with the structured guidance of a qualified teacher and the help of a wide range of learning support staff.

Under these circumstances, the task of leading learning will become very different. Such a change in schools will require a massive injection of resources, which the countries represented in this book should be able to afford, but many others will not. As the potential of information and communication technology offers greater possibilities for schools, the gap between education in the developed world and that in the developing countries will increase. The challenge is not only to prepare the leaders for the resource-rich school of the future, but also to use the power of technology to ensure that high quality education is more widely available. School leaders will become more internationally minded and will seek increased opportunities for mutually beneficial programmes between schools in different countries.

The National College for School Leadership will have an important role to play in developing this broader role and will be in a unique position to promote professional development opportunities internationally. The speed with which changes in education will occur and the variety of responses required of schools present an increasing challenge to school leaders, but the job of leadership will remain as fascinating as any occupation. The privilege of helping young people to develop and achieve their potential, the empowering of a group of intelligent professionals to give of their best and the positive influence on a local community combine to create the rich tapestry of leadership which is apparent from the 14 studies in this book.

Index